Numen
The Spiral Path

Elen Sentier

www.capallbann.co.uk

Numerology
The Spiral Path

ISBN 186163 270 3

Cover design by Paul Mason based on a picture by Elen Sentier

Published by:

Capall Bann Publishing
Auton Farm
Milverton
Somerset
TA4 1NE

To Lilla Bok, Barbara Somers and Ian Gordon-Brown

Contents

1

Numerology

Numbers are our connection to the universe. They are a shorthand or code which seems likely to be understood throughout the universe and scientists at SETI (Search for Extra-Terrestrial Investigation) send out messages to the rest of the universe in the hope of getting an answer. Numerologists use numbers to discover how people work, what makes them tick, because numbers are a code for all life.

Numbers, ratios, relationships between things, exist beyond human invention. The distance between the Earth and the Sun is so many miles, kilometres, light-years, whatever you like to name it … but the name doesn't *make* the number, it merely describes it and gives it a form which we can use. The distance was there before there were any human beings to give names to things.

Human beings have spent their whole collective life, several millions of Earth-years, in evolution, growing larger and more inclusive. We have been learning how to distinguish between unconscious herd behaviour and conscious group behaviour. We have been learning how to put the needs of others, including the planet, before our own personal needs and wants. This is a difficult thing to do – until reincarnation becomes a fact of life for you. Once you know, for certain, that this life is not all there is you begin to feel less pressured to get the most of everything, right now, for yourself. You can appreciate beginning things which will not come to fruition until long after the body you are currently wearing is dead and gone. You can even realise that you might come back in a future incarnation and see it.

This last has wonderful repercussions. If you are going to reincarnate, many times, then it's extremely likely you'll walk into the resultant mess some of your previous behaviour has initiated. Once we realise this, it's an excellent reason for not behaving badly in the first place! Humanity is coming to realise this now, at the beginning of the twenty-first century. Even if it's a bit of a dim glow to many as yet, it is happening, and the Three behind the Throne are now able to interact with human consciousness in a much more visible way. This reinforces our interconnectedness with all Life. It also enables us to realise that there's much more life than we may have thought, that what we have cheerfully called inanimate objects might not be so after all. There is soul, anima, in every form be it fridge, fir tree, fox or financial adviser.

The numbers of one's birth provide the clues to the pattern of that incarnation. Knowing the pattern enables us to bring more of it to light, to consciousness, and so helps us grow.

Bringing one's self to consciousness can be very difficult and painful. But, until we do, we have no chance of being WHOLE. We live in a world, and a universe, where duality is what makes Life possible, be you a star emitting light and so automatically creating shadow and dark, or a human being making love and creating a child.

Time
Time is different for all of us.

1. Day – the inmost point of the spiral.
Monday doesn't happen at the same time all around the

Earth. When your Monday begins depends on your degree of longitude, the moment the sun rises in your part of the world. Monday, for you in London, doesn't begin at the same time as it does for your friends in New York, Mexico City, Sydney or Cape Town. Or even your friends in Paris. Our time, our days, are always wholly related to where we live.

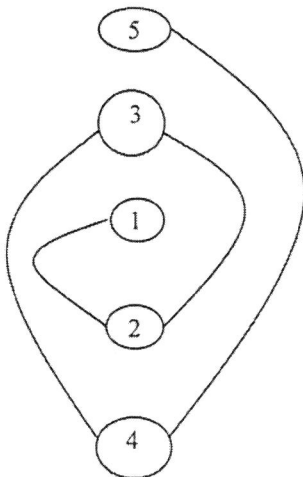

2. Month – the second turn of the spiral.

June doesn't begin precisely at the same time for you and all of your friends around the world either. However, it's a much longer period, thirty whole days-worth, so you all get to experience June together, at roughly the same time, even if it's not precisely the same moment.

3. Year – the third turn of the spiral.

Every year we all have new year celebrations, new calendars. Again, the actual moment when the new year arrives is different for all those friends around the world. But they all get to experience that year together for most of its three hundred and sixty-five (or six) days.

4. Century – the fourth turn of the spiral.

Every hundred years we reach a new century. Again we don't all do this at exactly the same moment but we have four human generations (a generation is calculated to be about twenty-five years) in which to experience a century.

Looking from the Earth's perspective, each century is like our annual birthday. Something happens for most of us, even if we try to suppress it, as we have our birthday each year. As the Planet has her hundred-year anniversary a similar change happens for her too. With each passing century the Planet goes through 1-ness, 2-ness, 3-ness etc. i.e. 19 = 1, 20 = 2, 21 = 3. and so on.

If you look at the changes and new beginnings which happened between 1900 and 1999 the sheer number is amazing. Additionally there was a tremendous population explosion of human beings – in 1900 there were just over one billion of us on the planet, in 1999 there were six billion! This has made a great difference to those of us born during this period, altered the way we perceive things, made great social changes, increased awareness of the effects people have on the planet, all sorts of things. So the century number 19 was very much about newness and change which is a major trait of the number 1 – what 19 adds down to.

Look at the attributes of each number and see how each century expresses those attributes. The century 1800-1899 has the attributes of 9. From 1700-1799 you are looking at 8, and so on. Read up about the history of those times and compare this to the number qualities it is illuminating.

The century-year sets the tone for that century ... 1900 = 1, 1800 = 9, 1700 = 8 and so on. Every ten years there's a sub-set of energy ... 2000 = 2, 2010 = 3, 2020 = 4. All the people born between 2000 and 2009 share a 2-ness of decade as those born between 2010 and 2019 share a 3-ness, but it goes further than that. The events of our lives which happen during those cycles share that number quality too. Numerology doesn't end when you're born, it's happening all the time. These ten year cycles are a part of the spiral of life, at 2010 we all move from a 2-ness which colours our lives into a 3-ness. Many of us older people will have "done 3-ness" before but never quite like this because there hasn't been a year 2010 in our recorded history.

Of course, the Earth is very much older than two thousand years but the particular cycle we are living in at the moment was conditioned and numbered by the emergence of the Christian faith. Although other traditions number things differently according to their own histories, as a world we are living with the Christian tradition. Think about it, if you catch a plane from London to Hong Kong you don't suddenly find yourself in a different year when you land. The Hong Kong newspapers will still have the same date on them that the London ones do ... the Hong Kong stock market wouldn't do business else. So, like it or not, we are living in the Christian era.

This moving up of the decade numbers each year, moving up an order of magnitude, is a part of how the spiral works.

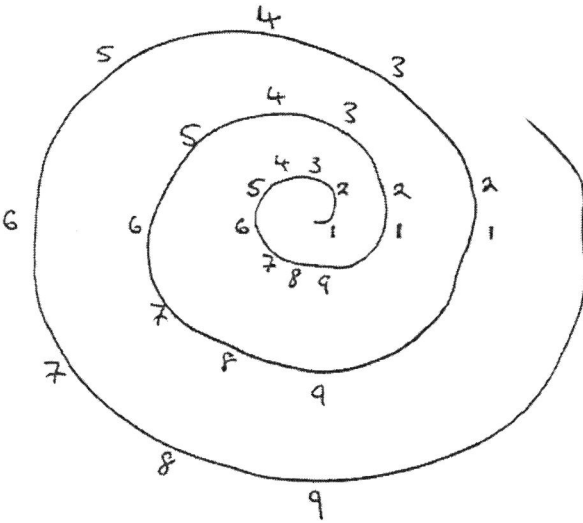

Each turn, of the spiral gets larger and more inclusive. This way, not only do we evolve but the planets and the gods do too.

There are three paths which human beings can follow.

• The straight or linear, past behind you, future in front of you.

• The circular where you tread around the route, returning to places, situations you've been to before.

• The spiral path on which you return to places that are *similar* to those you've been to before but are on another turn of the spiral.

On the spiral path, each time round, you include all you've learned since the last time a situation like this turned up. So it isn't the same place, situation. You have grown and, by doing so, enabled the space-time to grow too.

The spiral path connects you to the other worlds. The circular path gives you glimpses of them but you cannot really be there because you are returning, time on time, to places you have already been. The spiral path is the one which otherworldly beings tread.

We begin our personal evolution on the linear path, we progress from a to b to c and it seems like a time-line. Later, as we begin to feel the connectedness of every thing, we also sense the *homecoming* which is so reassuring at the end of our lives. We see our life as a circle, like Bilbo, there and back again. We go out on a journey and return home.

Later still, we begin to understand that we can only truly go home when we realise that home is a place we have never yet been, because the individual who returns home is not the same one as went out. That individual brings back all that they have gleaned from another lifetime, another incarnation, to add to the store of knowing held by the home. So we come to know the spiral path, for the home we return to is not the one we left, nor are we the same being who returns to it.

This can be a difficult concept to accept because it shows, unutterably, the impermanence of things and people. It shows you can never go back. It makes us know that loss is real and always, always happens. The child or teenager or young adult can no longer play in the garden of happy-ever-after. Now the garden has to include the whole world. Eventually it will include the whole of creation.

So the child-soul walks the straight path. The young-adult-soul walks the circular path. The mature soul walks the spiral path.

5. Millennium – the fifth turn of the spiral.

In the year 2000 we got to experience three things at once … a new year, a new century and a new millennium – millennium means one thousand years. Again, all the millennium parties began at their own individual moments when that part of the Earth moved into the new century and millennium. A thousand years is far longer than the human lifespan although some other life-forms, some trees, live several thousand years. It is good to imagine how they see the changes in life that happen over their lifetimes.

Each of these points, moments of change, are determined for us here on Earth by our planet's movement around the sun. They are also determined by our sun's (the *star* for this solar system) movement within our home galaxy, the Milky Way. They are further determined by the movement, dance, of our galaxy within the whole cosmos, for our galaxy moves, dances, with all the other galaxies in the universe.
We determine planting, animal husbandry, harvests, food

production, through calendars – ways of showing what time we are in. In the miniature timescale of a day we determine when we get up, go to work, have a lunch break, come home, catch a train, watch TV, go to bed. We do this by knowing where our planet is relative to the sun and the stars … however we mostly don't think of it that way.

We count the days, months and years, give them numbers, and so we know how old we are, how long we've been in a relationship, had the car, when the cat's birthday is, when the rent/mortgage gets paid, when we'll retire – all that stuff. And perhaps we have an idea that all these numbers have some significance, even if we pooh-pooh it and laugh at ourselves (embarrassedly) when we're with friends and family.

Enjoy the walk through the spiral of Time.

Duality

Duality often has a bad press but everything has a shadow and without this shadow it would have no form, we would not be able to see it. Ursula le Guinn puts this beautifully in LEFT HAND OF DARKNESS … *[my embolding]*

… Towards the middle of Nimmer, after much wind and bitter cold, we came into a quiet weather for many days. If there was storm it was far south of us, down there, and we inside the blizzard had only an all but windless overcast. At first the over cast was thin, so that the air was vaguely radiant with an even, sourceless sunlight reflected from both clouds and snow, from above and below. Overnight the weather thickened somewhat. All brightness was gone leaving nothing. We stepped out of the tent onto nothing. Sledge and tent were there, Estraven stood beside me, **but neither he nor I cast any shadow.** *There was dull light all around, everywhere. When he walked on the crisp snow* **no shadow showed the footprint. We left no track.**

Without shadow the travellers can see nothing, distinguish nothing, cannot place themselves in the landscape. So it is in life. We need the shadow in order to find ourselves and where we are in our lives, in our relationships with people and things. We need duality, self and shadow, in order to realise existence.

In order to work with your numbers it's necessary to grow into the concept that shadow is an integral part of the whole. This does not mean that being selfish and mean is acceptable, nor any of the other human traits which don't make for harmonious relationships. But it does mean that the shadow is necessary to enable the whole to grow. As human beings, we work between light and dark, constantly moving between them weaving the patterns of life.

Another way of looking at the concept of shadow is through the story of Peter Pan. This was written by a theosophist who put the whole allegory together to show many spiritual points. Peter Pan had had his shadow cut off when he was a baby and ran away to play with the Lost Boys. As long as he had no shadow he could never grow up. That is true for all of us. If we refuse (cut off) our shadow then we too cannot grow up. We all know old age pensioners who still have an emotional age of five, with concomitant irresponsibility. In the story, Peter Pan gets Wendy to sew his shadow back on and so is able to return to the everyday world. He doesn't find this altogether easy or attractive as he quickly becomes accountable and responsible for his actions. This is painful, but it is the only way to become whole.

Being whole is about living an *and/and* life. Most of us somehow find ourselves living exclusive, *either/or* lives. We don't naturally include. It's an awkward trap. We need to be able to distinguish between self and other, but it's not advantageous to shut ourselves within a box and only accept what fits there with our current opinions.

In tai chi, except at the beginning and end, you are never "double weighted", never have your weight equally in both feet. If you do you are immobile, you cannot move. In order to move you have to shift your weight more into one foot than the other. Then you can lift the lighter foot, then you can move. This is a form of balance, and of grounding, which is less common in our thinking. The balance must be there or you won't be able to shift your weight, but you cannot move if you are firmly planted on both feet. Duality holds this quality of movement which is vital to living.

Another way of looking at it is to think of a coin. The coin has a head and a tail, two sides. It is one whole coin *only* when it has both sides of its self, and so are we. Without both sides there would be no coin, no WHOLENESS. We struggle with this, it's not how our education and morality systems teach us things are, or should be, so it requires lots of mind-stretching. But mind-stretching is fun.

Your numbers bring all this to light within you so that you can see, know, understand and internalise their qualities, realise your true self. This is the self, the personality, the grail-cup, which your soul built out of the matter of the planet, as a vehicle, home, space-suit for getting about on Planet Earth. As you come to know this vehicle so your soul-self can inhabit it more easily, work it so that you are able to do your soul-work. This is the most satisfying thing in the world. Gradually, you come to know yourself as the soul and no longer need to identify yourself as your personality. This has massive advantages ...

• You no longer fear death. You know, absolutely, that you have incarnated in many bodies, of many races, and that you will do so many times again.

• You know you are never alone. You remember how it has been before. You know you have friends and work-mates who are not presently incarnate but you can converse with them across the worlds. And they can help you.

• If you fear neither death nor loneliness you are less likely to be selfish. In consequence you won't start wars (street-size or country-size).

• You won't work in competition with other people, so all the ills of advertising, normality, one-up-man-ship, scoring, peer pressure, et al, won't exist for you. If these cease to exist for enough people then whole industries which contribute to harming the planet will die of neglect.

Becoming whole helps the whole planet and everything that lives and breathes and has its being thereon.

2

The Spiral Dance

The numbers work in pairs.

SOUL CENTRED			PERSONALITY CENTRED
Ancestors	8	1	Body/ego/will
Love/Wisdom	7	2	Feelings
Knowing	6	3	Thinking
Soul-Purpose	5	4	Intuition

• Note each of these pairs adds to 9, the number or power, of potential.

We can look at the numbers in terms of the four subtle bodies and Jung's four functions ... Sensory, Feeling, Thinking and Intuitive.

At the centre we have the 9 and the zero, the power and the container/ mirror, the energy behind manifestation and so also behind incarnation. Each of the arms of the cross holds one of the subtle bodies with its associated function.

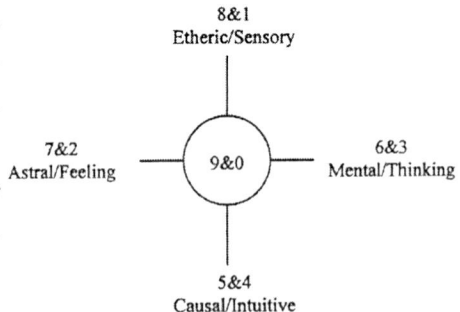

```
                    8&1
                 Etheric/Sensory
                      |
                      |
   7&2            ( 9&0 )           6&3
Astral/Feeling                  Mental/Thinking
                      |
                      |
                    5&4
                 Causal/Intuitive
```

NOTE – the numbers don't represent *either/or* on the subtle bodies and functions. 7&2 *both* contain the principles of the astral body and of the feeling function, it's not 7=astral and 2=feelings, 7 and 2 *together* hold the energy of the astral body, which is one of the four parts of the personality body (see The Soul as Builder in Chapter 1), and of the feeling function. Similarly with the other three pairs of numbers and their associated subtle bodies and functions.

Each pair of numbers on the arms of the cross add to 9, the number which is at the centre along with the zero, and we've gone into this wholeness earlier. When the birth and name numbers add to 9 they give a special power to the person and they show their focused line of attention for the lifetime.

Involution & Evolution

This drawing shows the numbers spiralling out clockwise from zero at the centre until you come to 4/5. Here they change and reverse the spiral, going back inwards, anticlockwise, to the centre from 5 to 9.

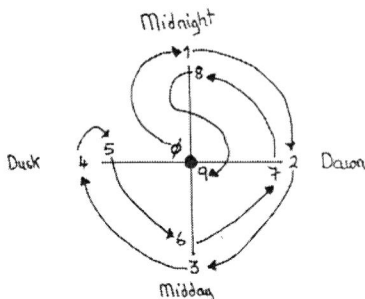

These two spirals symbolise evolution, the outward, clockwise, spiral and involution, the inward, anticlockwise, spiral. On the outward journey the person strives towards something more, higher, than themselves. On the inward journey they take what they have garnered and use it for the good of the earth and their fellow humans.

This table shows some basic features of involution and evolution.

INVOLUTION	EVOLUTION
Heaven → Earth	Earth → Heaven
Widdershins	Deosil
Anticlockwise	Clockwise
Centripetal	Centrifugal
Breathing IN	Breathing OUT
Midday → Midnight	Midnight → Midday

Of course, you are never only going one way. You may be concentrating on evolution at any stage but, at the same time, you will also be working to help your fellows and your planet. Or vice versa, you may be deeply involved in helping others but your own evolution doesn't stop even if it is in background mode. The two journeys facilitate each other. By working on your own evolution you find yourself in places where others need your help and by working to help others you will find

14

they show you things which make you grow. The inward and outward journeys spiral together like the two fishes in the Yin Yang diagram.

The Chinese astronomers watched the positions of the constellation of the Bear in the sky and measured the shadow of the sun, marked the positions of the solstices and equinoxes, and saw the seasonal changes and related them to them. In the northern hemisphere when the Bear points to the east it's spring, pointing to the south and it's summer, when it points to the west it's autumn and the north is winter. There are similar observations for the southern hemisphere.

Allen Tsai has done some excellent work on this, see his diagram:

Alan says …

By observing the cycle of the Sun, we can use a pole, post at right angles to the ground, and record the lengths of the shadow about every 15 days for a year. The shortest shadow is found on the day of Summer Solstice in China. The longest shadow is found on the day of Winter Solstice. The day of Winter Solstice has the least sunshine in the year. After Winter Solstice, the day will gain more sunshine each day till Summer Solstice. We can say Yang begins right after Winter Solstice and Yin begins right after Summer Solstice in the northern hemisphere.

After recording 24 shadow lines, we move the lines into the diagram of six concentric circles with 24 sectors beginning from Winter Solstice to Summer Solstice. The length of each line will subtract the portion of the length of Summer Solstice shadow line because we want to give Summer Solstice maximum Yang.

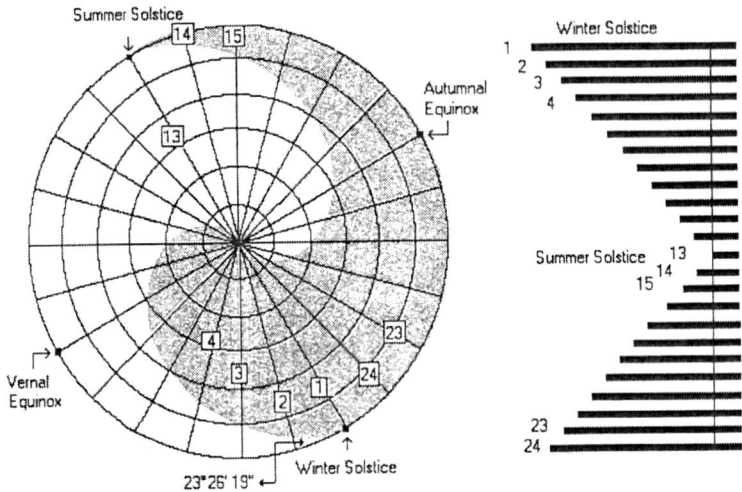

Summer Solstice
14 15
Autumnal Equinox
13
Winter Solstice
1
2
3
4
Summer Solstice 13
14
15
23
24
4
23
3
24
1
2
Vernal Equinox
23° 26' 19"
Winter Solstice

From Winter Solstice to Summer Solstice, the shadow lines are drawn from the centre of the circle to the boundary. From Summer Solstice to Winter Solstice, the shadow lines are drawn from circle boundary to the centre, because ancient Chinese believed that Chi Energy goes different directions right after Summer Solstice and Winter Solstice. Next, we can connect all the lines and dim the shadow lines (Yin) part, the Ying Yang symbol appears.

Again, these spirals go inward and outward through the year, like breathing. To return to the numbers, the out-breathing, evolutionary cycle goes from zero to four, the in-breathing, involutionary cycle goes from five to nine. These cycles are important. You need to breath out in order to breath in, and to breathe in in order to breathe out, so it is with numbers and with your life.

The numbers also relate to the three strands of the Caduceus staff, the Ida, Pingala and Sushumna. The numbers 1-4 make up the evolutionary snake which travels up the staff. The numbers 5-8 make up the involutionary snake which travels down the staff. The staff itself is the numbers 9 and 0. The in-breath draws energy from heaven to earth, involution. The out-breath draws energy from earth to heaven, evolution.

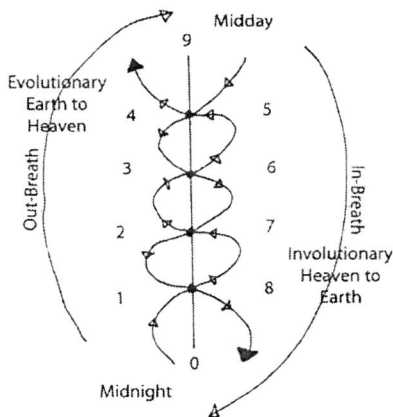

Soul & Personality

• PERSONALITY centred qualities are EVOLUTIONARY. The personality needs to evolve, to become inclusive rather than separatist. Individuation must take place, which is very different from egocentricity. The personal self rises up from earth to heaven.

• SOUL centred qualities are INVOLUTIONARY, this because the soul knows that its job is to turn back, away from home, and to help those walking the path behind them. What they have gained they now give back, so they turn away from personal evolution to help their fellows on the path. The soul-self comes down from heaven to earth.

Evolution is about striving to become a complete person, and so a good vehicle for your soul to use in this incarnation.

Involution is about returning to Earth in order to help others, as well as growing more one's self. Usually people need to make a certain amount of growth before they are ready to turn back from paradise for the sake of the world, but all of us do this to some degree although we may not be aware of it.

Soul and personality work together on these jobs even if they seem, at first, to be contradictory. Bringing together apparent pairs of opposites is what our universe is about. It works on the principle of relationship, duality, I and thou. The patterns of the numbers shows this and seeing this helps us find ways to bring the opposites together within ourselves

The Soul as Builder

In order to work with your numbers it's useful to have a grasp of spiritual engineering, how the personality is constructed, by whom and for what purpose.

You may already realise that there are no conscripts to incarnation ... only volunteers! You-the-Soul created the *vessel* in which it can live for the incarnation. It also created the job-plan which it hopes to achieve in the incarnation, with the help of the *vessel* it has created. This *vessel* is also called the GOLDEN CUP or GRAIL and is your personality body.

Your soul decides, in concert with its soul group, on the job it wishes to do in each incarnation. It needs a *personality* to function on this (or any other) planet. This is the vessel, vehicle, golden cup or grail which holds it. To make this, it goes to the planet on which it has decided to incarnate and asks the planet if it can have some planetary matter with which to build its vehicle. It must be made from the matter of the planet it's going to live on or, like an organ transplant, it'll get rejected. So what happens?

To build your PHYSICAL-SENSING body, the soul builds a blueprint (the etheric body), then borrows physical and etheric matter and builds your physical body out of it.

To build your ASTRAL/EMOTIONAL body, it borrows planetary emotional matter and builds your emotional body (astral body).

To build your MENTAL/THINKING body, it borrows planetary mental matter and builds your thinking body (mental body)

To build your INTUITIVE/SOUL-BODY body, it borrows planetary causal matter and builds your soul-body (causal body). The causal or soul body is the recorder for the life – your hard disc on which all your life-experience is recorded. When you die it is input into the ancestral cauldron. It also holds your life-intent (job) for this incarnation. NB – the causal body is NOT your soul.

Then the soul pours the whole lot into the alchemical flask of your mother's womb, brews it for nine months, sparks it – i.e. jumps in and en-souls it, at around 3 months gestation. Then, at birth-time, the soul stirs your mother's womb to begin labour.

End result: YOU – a flesh-covered personality with a soul waiting to come through!

Your soul has to wait until your personality is sufficiently "grown up" to be able to communicate with it. It is the personality which contacts the soul, *not* the other way round. The soul has to wait "in meditation deep" to quote a master. It cannot be the first to make contact, the personality must open the door.

Later, at the end of your incarnation, it is your soul who knows when it's time to pull the life-cord out of your heart and bring you to death, usually because you've finished the job. Even if the manner of your death appears to be an accident it's very possible the accident was intentional in order for more lessons to be learned by all involved in it. Things practically never happen just to you, there are always others involved and their soul-learning is just as important as yours. What happens to you can equally be of benefit to them. Life and death are inclusive.

At death the planetary matter your soul used is returned to the Earth, hopefully in a *more evolved state* than when your soul borrowed it. This is your MAJOR way of doing planetary healing: borrowing planetary matter to live in and handing it back in better shape when you die.

It's part of your soul's bargain with the planet. If you haven't evolved, grown personally, hopefully even become an integrated personality, then the planetary matter loaned to your soul could be in the same, or even in a worse, state than when your soul borrowed it some three-score-years-and-ten ago. You can imagine your soul having to apologise to the Earth for such an event! Try not to let it happen ...

Think of it this way ...

• At first you're only conscious of your *personal self.*

• As you grow more aware you *change your seat* to that of the soul and, by changing your seat, your perspective, you see things as the soul – a wider view than the personal self alone has.

• But you see *through the LENS of the personality* which enables you to speak and be heard in the world. Souls don't make sense in the everyday world.

• You don't lose your personal viewpoint in order to gain the soul's, you ADD to it by making your personal self large and inclusive enough to encompass both. The integrated personality becomes the LENS which focuses both itself and the soul.

• At death you return the planetary matter you've used. By refining the material your soul borrows in each incarnation you "heal", make more whole, the planet.

The Integrated Personality
The personality is integrated when the four subtle bodies are all aligned and working together. This happens when the chakras are also aligned and working together. You read about the four subtle bodies in the Soul as Builder. They are made from planetary matter, the stuff of the subtle bodies of the planet, and they correlate to the four elements of earth, water, air and fire. They also correlate to Jung's four functions. The are ...

SUBTLE BODY	ELEMENT	JUNG'S FUNCTION
Etheric	Earth	Sensing/physical
Astral	Water	Feeling self
Mental	Air	Thinking/intellectual self
Causal	Fire	Intuitive self

The simplest way to begin to get to know them and work with them is using Jung's functions as we're usually reasonably aware of these.

SENSATION is related to touch, sight, smell, hearing, taste, bodily sensations like hot and cold, pain and pleasure. It's about the body and it *knows*. The body holds a great deal of knowledge, as well as learned responses to various situations like pulling your hand away from a flame or running like hell if a sabre-tooth tiger is after you. It also knows more subtle things, through the etheric body, like when people are lying to you, when they are sad or happy or angry.

We're also reasonably au fait with FEELINGS. We all have them, we all have emotions, and we're reasonably used to

21

them although some people are more emotionally literate than others. It is important, in getting to know yourself, to learn the difference between the "feeling" when somebody is lying to you – which is likely coming from body-knowing – and the feeling of sadness or happiness which you may pick up empathically from others.

THINKING is something we're usually quite proud of, even if we may not actually be rocket-science material. We learn to think and to reason fairly early on. If we keep at it we can get quite good at the process of "if – then", i.e. making logical connections between things. This is a very useful trait to develop in spiritual work and will aid you in discerning when your intuition is working and when it's wishful thinking. The thinking self is the rational part of us, it helps us get up in the morning, cook supper, catch the right train, drive the car. It's not so good at "knowing", that's a different part of the self which is usually best contacted, at first, through body-knowing.

INTUITION ... can be a difficult one as we're so often educated to be rational above all things. We're encouraged to need everything to be proved, to believe what's written in books or told us by somebody with alphabet soup after their name. We tend to pooh-pooh our own hunches, as we call them, preferring to believe in "coincidence", whilst not really understanding what that word means.

These four bodies need to be working together in harmony, each one functioning at the right moment in appropriate ways. That doesn't mean equally balanced at all times. It's not a lot of good trying to have a rational argument with a hungry crocodile who is only interested in you as lunch. Turn your thinking process onto seeing the quickest way out of there and your sensory function onto making your legs run faster than an Olympic sprinter. You can have your panic feelings later too, when you're well away from there and in a safe place to cry into a cup of tea. And as far as your intuition is concerned forget it, it obviously wasn't working well enough … or you've not learned to listen to it … which is why you ended up as potential crocodile-lunch in the first place. Sort that out a lot later!

When your subtle bodies are aligned and working properly you'll be able to fit actions to situations and behave appropriately. The surest way of knowing when they are aligned is being able to recognise when you're acting appropriately and when you're not.

Aligning your chakras... what's this about?

There are seven major chakras as you probably know. There are lots more minor ones and even more mini ones but we're not going into those here. The seven major ones work in three pairs with the Brow as the overall "control centre". The chakras work together as follows …

Crown with Base
Throat with Sacral
Heart with Solar Plexus

The Brow carries the energies of the other chakras in their masculine and feminine energy forms in its pair of petals. It is the organisational centre.

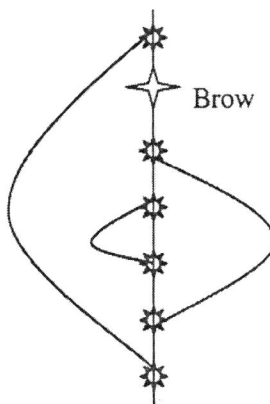

Brow

This book is not about how to align your chakras, there are lots of ways of doing this, look around bookshops, try some workshops, and try the exercises in this book. Ten to one your body and soul know the best way for you to do this, better than all your friends and other people who may want to advise you.

3

The Patterns of the Numbers

The numbers work in pairs ...

8 with 1
7 with 2
6 with 3
5 with 4.

Zero actually never appears on its own in any of the times-tables but only as a compound number, with another number, e.g. 10, 20, 30, etc. The numbers pairs show evolution and involution in the patterns they make, but to see how they do this you have to recall your times-tables, remember ...

Once three is three
Two threes are six
Three threes are nine ... and so on.

You'll find the tables set out with each pair of numbers. First of all let's look at them, take this example ...

5X		FINAL			4X
		NUMBER			
1x5=5		5	4		1x4=4
2x5=10	1+0=1	1	8		2x4=8
3x5=15	1+5=6	6	3	1+2=3	3x4=12
4x5=20	2+0=2	2	7	1+6=7	4x4=16
5x5=25	2+5=7	7	2	2+0=2	5x4=20
6x5=30	3+0=3	3	6	2+4=6	6x4=24
7x5=35	3+5=8	8	1	2+8=10, 1+0=1	7x4=28
8x5=40	4+0=4	4	5	3+2=5	8x4=32

• Put your left forefinger on the TOP of the left-hand "Final Number" column, on the 5.

• Put your right-hand forefinger on BOTTOM of the right-hand "Final Number" column, also on the 5.

• Now, come *down* with the left hand and go *up* with the right hand, row by row.

• Your left forefinger goes down next to 1, while your right forefinger goes up to 1. Then the left forefinger goes down to 6 and the right forefinger goes up to 6.

• Keep doing this until your left forefinger is at the bottom and your right at the top. Then do it again in reverse, just to convince your mind of what's happened.

The numbers of the result of the 5-times and 4-times tables, when reduced to single figures, reverse each other like the diagram of the diagram of the Caduceus staff spirals in the last chapter. The numbers going UP are the EVOLUTIONARY spiral. The numbers going DOWN are the INVOLUTIONARY spiral.

You will see how they produce these spirals on the Numbers Circle.

We only go to 8x5 and 8x4 because 9 times anything reduces back to 9 – try it for yourself.

Look at this table. The first four rows reverse the second four rows. Involution and evolution again.

$$9 \times 9 = 81 \quad 8 + 1 = 9$$
$$9 \times 8 = 72 \quad 7 + 2 = 9$$
$$9 \times 7 = 63 \quad 6 + 3 = 9$$
$$9 \times 6 = 54 \quad 5 + 4 = 9$$

$$9 \times 5 = 45 \quad 4 + 5 = 9$$
$$9 \times 4 = 36 \quad 3 + 6 = 9$$
$$9 \times 3 = 27 \quad 2 + 7 = 9$$
$$9 \times 2 = 18 \quad 1 + 8 = 9$$

And ... the result of 9x9 is the reverse of the result of 9x2; the result of 9x8 is the reverse of the result of 9x3; the result of 9x7 is the reverse of the result of 9x4; and the result of 9x6 is the reverse of the result of 9x5.

There seems to be quite a pattern here, and it all seems to be about reversals, one going one way while its partner goes the other.

Furthermore, 10 times anything just adds a zero to the number

$$10 \times 5 = 50 \quad 5 + 0 = 5$$
$$10 \times 4 = 40 \quad 4 + 0 = 4$$

So 10 times anything when added down, reverts to the original number, but up an order of magnitude, up a turn of the spiral.

26

Although all this sounds rather heady and mind-boggling it works out in the actual numerology. Lets look at the patterns the numbers make.

Draw a circle, as in this diagram, and mark it with the numbers as shown.

o NB – 9 must be at the top

The other numbers pair, one on each side of the circle as shown. Because no addition of numbers ever reduces to zero there's no place for 0 on the numbers circle, there's no reason for it to be there.

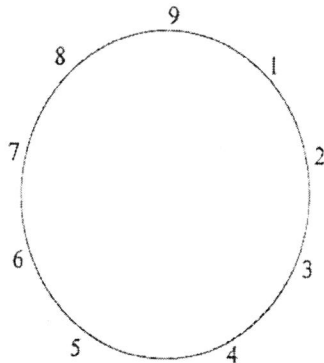

We are going to look at the patterns the times-tables make for each of the numbers. You'll see that each pair makes a pattern specific to themselves and that each member of a pair makes that pattern by going round the circle in the opposite way to its partner. Remember what we said about involution and evolution, widdershins and deosil, anti-clockwise and clockwise, how the shadows form the spiral curves on the yin-yang diagram, the centripetal and centrifugal paths and the planetary in and out breathing. This duality, in-breathing and

Troytown or Celtic maze

out-breathing, has been known for a very long time. The Troytown or Celtic maze is at least four thousand years old, its inward and outward paths show the double spiral pattern. Nowadays we see this in the double helix of DNA.

Circles 8 & 1

8X			FINAL NUMBER		1X
1x8=8			8	1	1x1=1
2x8=16	1+6=7		7	2	2x1=2
3x8=24	2+4=6		6	3	3x1=3
4x8=32	3+2=5		5	4	4x1=4
5x8=40	4+0=4		4	5	5x1=5
6x8=48	4+8=12	1+2=3	3	6	6x1=6
7x8=56	5+6=11	1+1=2	2	7	7x1=7
8x8=64	6+4=1		1	8	8x1=8
9x8=72	7+2=9		9	9	9x1=9
10x8=80	8+0=8		8	1	10x1=101+0=1

• Take the 8-times table first, the Soul-self and Involutionary spiral.

On your circle, put your pen on the 8 and draw a line to the 7, from 7 go to 6, from 6 to 5, from 5 to 4, from 4 to 3, from 3 to 2, from 2 to 1, from 1 to 9 and from 9 back home to 8 again..

You've drawn a circle-like form. Your pen has gone round *widdershins*, anti-clockwise, the opposite way round to the sun. This direction draws you down into the Earth, the *involutionary* spiral of the soul-centred one who turns back to help those on the path.

• Now take the 1-times table – the Personality and Evolutionary spiral.

Draw the numbers-circle again and go round the circle from 1, to 2, 3, 4, 5, 6, 7, 8, 9, 10 – the ten reducing to 1.

Again you've drawn a rough circle. This time your pen went round *deosil*, clockwise, sunwise. This circle takes you up from the Earth to Heaven. It is *the evolutionary spiral* of the personality which reaches out to find something greater than self, to become inclusive.

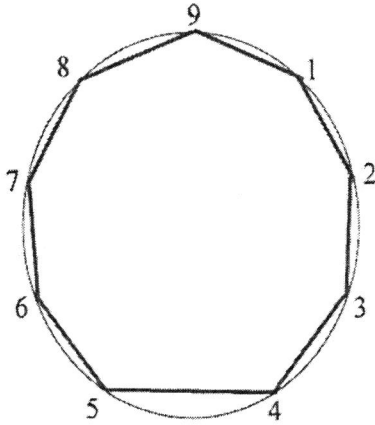

Pentagons 7 & 2

7X			FINAL NUMBER		2X	
1x7=7			7	2	1x2=2	
2x7=14	1+4=5		5	4	2x2=4	
3x7=21	2+1=3		3	6	3x2=6	
4x7=28	2+8=10	1+0=1	1	8	4x2=8	
5x7=35	3+5=8		8	1	5x2=10 1+0=1	
6x7=42	4+2=6		6	3	6x2=12	1+2=3
7x7=49	4+9=13	1+3=4	4	5	7x2=14	1+4=5
8x7=56	5+6=11	1+1=2	2	7	8x2=16	1+6=7
9x7=63	6+3=9		9	9	9x2=18	1+8=9
10x7=70	7+0=7		7	2	10x2=20	2+0=7

• Take the 7-times table first, the Soul-self and Involutionary spiral.

Do the pattern for the 7-times table. As before, put your pen on the 7, from 7 to 5, from 5 to 3, from 3 to 1, from 1 to 8, from 8 to 6, from 6 to 4, from 4 to 2, from 2 to 9 and from 9 back home to 7 again.

Again ... 7, is the way of the *involutionary spiral,* of the soul-centred one who turns back to help those on the

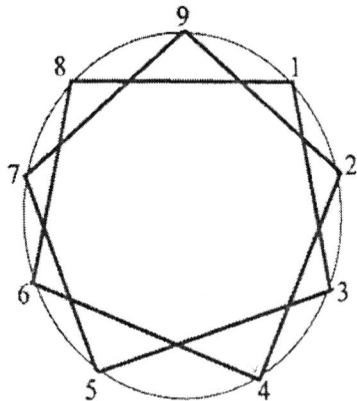

path … your pen went round *widdershins*, drawing you back down into the Earth.

• Now take the 2-times table – the Personality and Evolutionary spiral.

Put your pen on 2, from 2 to 4, from 4 to 6, from 6 to 8, from 8 to 1, from 1 to 3, from 3 to 5, from 5 to 7, from 7 to 9 and from 9 back home again to 2.

You went deosil this time, the evolutionary spiral around the pentagrams, the personality centred one reaching to become inclusive.

Triangles 6 & 3

The 6 and 3 times tables form triangles, three triangles, emphasising its three-ness three times. Try this exercise now to give yourself a feel of what it's about.

Torch Exercise

You need –

• 3 torches or spot lamps; light sources that will create a spot of light on the wall.
• a white wall or other un-coloured surface; it doesn't have to be very big.
• *red, blue* and *green* gel, as used in theatre lighting preferably.
• some means of holding all 3 torches/spot-lamps so the 3 spots play on the same spot on the wall, overlapping each other.
• Cover each light with gel, one red, one blue and one green.
• Set them up to point at one spot on the wall. When you've got this right ...
• Turn them on *one at a time* and watch how the colour of the light changes.
• With all three on you have WHITE LIGHT.
• Pass your hand between the torches and the wall.
• What happens on the wall?
• What happens on your hand?

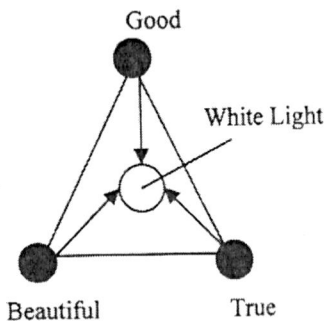

By moving your hand between the wall and the light source you created the rainbow. Think about this! White light was transformed into all the colours of life by your movement and interaction with both the Source and the Reflector. The movement causes shadows, rainbow shadows. By living, moving and having your being you refract etheric light into the myriad colours and create the present, the future, the past. By *living between* the light-source and the reflective surface you create the infinite *rainbow shadows* of Life.

But let's get back to the tables ...

6X		FINAL NUMBER		3X	
1x6=6		6	3	1x3=3	
2x6=12	1+2=3	3	6	2x3=6	
3x6=18	1+8=9	9	9	3x3=9	
4x6=24	2+4=6	6	3	4x3=12	1+2=3
5x6=30	3+0=3	3	6	5x3=15	1+5=6
6x6=36	3+6=9	9	9	6x3=18	1+8=9
7x6=42	4+2=6	6	3	7x3=21	2+1=9
8x6=48	4+8=12 1+2=3	3	6	8x3=24	2+4=6
9x6=54	5+4=9	9	9	9x3=27	2+7=9
10x6=60	6+0=6	6	3	10x3=30	3+0=7

• Take the 6-times table first, the Soul-self and Involutionary spiral.

For the 6-times table put your pen on the 6, go to 3, then to 9 and from 9 back to 6. Then you do it again, twice more. Three triangles, one on top of the other. And all going widdershins, the involutionary spiral.

• Now take the 3-times table – the Personality and Evolutionary spiral.

For the 3-times table, going deosil, the evolutionary spiral, put your pen on the 3, then go to 6, then to 9, then back to 3. Three times.

Spend time pondering this pattern, remember the torch exercise.

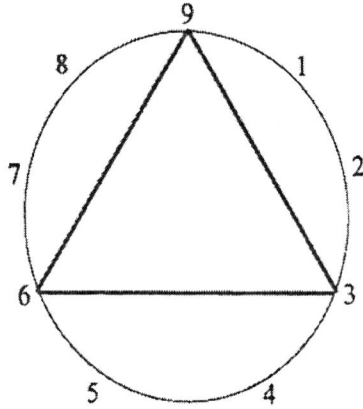

Stars 5 & 4

5X		FINAL NUMBER		4X	
1x5=5		5	4	1x4=4	
2x5=10	1+0=1	1	8	2x4=8	
3x5=15	1+5=6	6	3	3x4=12	1+2=3
4x5=20	2+0=2	2	7	4x4=16	1+6=7
5x5=25	2+5=7	7	2	5x4=20	2+0=2
6x5=30	3+0=3	3	6	6x4=24	2+4=6
7x5=35	3+5=8	8	1	7x4=28	2+8=10 1+0=1
8x5=40	4+0=4	4	5	8x4=32	3+2=5
9x5=45	4+5=9	9	9	9x4=36	3+6=9
10x5=50	5+0=5	5	4	10x4=40	4+0=4

• Take the 5-times table first, the Soul-self and Involutionary spiral.

So round you go, widdershins, the involutionary direction, from 5 to 1, 1 to 6, 6 to 2, 2 to 7, 7 to 3, 3 to 8, 8 to 4, 4 to 9 and 9 back home to 5 again, Making a beautiful nine-pointed star.

• Now take the 4-times table – the Personality and Evolutionary spiral.

Again going deosil, sun-wise ... put your pen on the 4, from 4 to 8, 8 to 3, 3 to 7, 7 to 2, 2 to 6, 6 to 1, 1 to 5, 5 to 9 and from 9 back home to 4, making the 9-pointed star again, in the evolutionary direction.

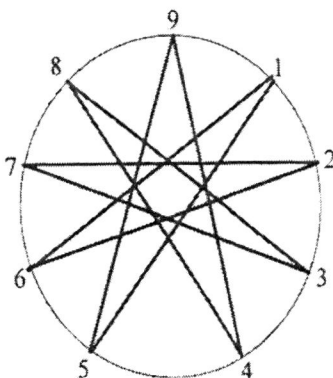

The Sun Symbol 9 & O

Nine and zero are different ...

9X		FINAL		0X
		NUMBER		
1x9=9		9	0	1x0=0
2x9=18	1+8=9	9	0	2x0=0
3x9=27	2+7=9	9	0	3x0=0
4x9=36	3+6=9	9	0	4x0=0
5x9=45	4+5=9	9	0	5x0=0
6x9=54	4+5=9	9	0	6x0=0
7x9=63	6+3=9	9	0	7x0=0
8x9=72	7+2=9	9	0	8x0=0
9x9=81	8+1=9	9	0	9x0=0
10x9=90	9+0=9	9	0	10x0=0

As you see, both tables only ever reduce to themselves. There is something fundamental about them which is significant when you work with them. The occultist, Helena Blavatsky, described creation as follows ...

- At first there is the point   •

- The point vibrates, becoming a line |

- It vibrates more, becoming the cross   +

- Which expands to become the universe   ⊕

Blavatsky calls this *cosmogenesis*. The line within the circle is called the *duration*, the ratio of its length to the circumference of the circle (pi, π) is the number of creative beings involved in the making of that universe. So each universe has a number too. When you come to the end of the line it is a death and a new beginning.

This is like the 9 and the 0.

For the 9-times table, your pen just keeps on dotting on the figure nine, it doesn't make the usual involutionary and evolutionary circles. And the zero doesn't even appear on the numbers circle at all. You can take it as no-thing and express that as a circle. If you put the symbols for the 9 and the 0 together, as a picture, you get the glyph for the sun.

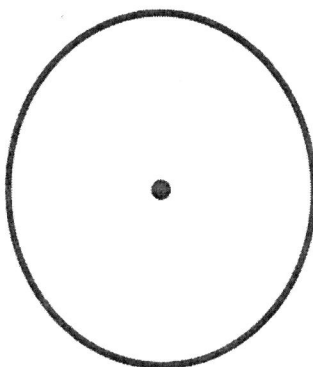

Nine is the power which enables the sun, symbolised by the dot at its centre. Zero is the container which holds that power.

If you add any number to nine and then reduce it back down you will always get the number you first thought of. It's as if the nine is invisible. For instance …

5+9 = 14   1+4 = 5   or

2+5+6+7+9 = 29 2+9 = 11 1+1 = 2

Try it out for yourself, you'll find that whatever you add to the nine it always disappears. Another nice trick of the 9-times table is that it goes up so far and then reverses. In doing so, it creates the pairs of numbers.

9 is fundamental in creating the numbers, it's the power behind them and the expression of their wholeness. It creates

them, in their pairs, and each pair of numbers holds its own individual pattern of duality. 9 requires to be broken down into the pairs in order to create a pattern. Of itself, 9 is the dot, it has no relationship to anything but itself and the circle. In order to move, create pattern and life, 9 has to split into other numbers. This is like the Torch Exercise. The white light on the wall has to refract, through the agency of your hand moving between the light-source and the wall. The 9 too has to refract in order to become visible through the other numbers.

09	90
18	81
27	72
36	63
45	54

Look at the first column here. You go *down* from 1 times 9 to 5 times nine with the numbers one way round then, at 6 time 9 the numbers reverse, go *up* the other way round. Five nines are forty-five (45), then six nines are fifty-four (54). Note too that the 9-times table holds each of the pairs of numbers, 9/0, 8/1, 7/2, 6/3, 5/4.

9 holds both the powers of involution and evolution.

0	9
1	8
2	7
3	6
4	5
5	4
6	3
7	2
8	1
9	0

Write down, in a column, the numbers zero to nine (0,1,2,3,4,5,6,7,8,9). Then, in another column to its left, write down the number nine to zero (9,8,7,6,5,4,3,2,1,0). What have you got? The results of the 9-times table!

So nine does its involution and evolution in hidden ways, evolves and involves through the actual making of its numbers.

With zero whatever you add, subtract, multiply or divide it with or to you still end up with zero, nothing, no-thing. So zero is about no-thing-ness. It contains the potential for all things.

You've seen, and actually drawn, the patterns the numbers make, the spiral inwards and then the spiral outwards. Drawing it puts the sense *into your body*, begins your body-knowing of the numbers and this is very important. You need to understand numerology intellectually but you will never know it until you have also acquired the body-knowing. This is an instinctual process. Becoming accustomed to working with your instincts enables your intuition to function ... and you to be aware of it. People often find it difficult to be sure when they are truly being intuitive and when it's just wishful thinking – this is where body-knowing helps you. Your body doesn't work with the intellectual intricacies that your brain does. It knows when it's wet, hot, thirsty, hungry, sexy, it doesn't need to intellectualise about these things it just *knows* them and it can show you, through sensation, when you are working authentically and when you're shamming, but you need to learn its language.

9-ness and the Soul

The soul sits at the 3rd point of the triangle, between the pairs of numbers. It needs to partake of both energies of both halves of each number pair in order to be whole. It needs to add to 9.

To be a complete, soul-infused person we need both our outer, visible number and its shadow. As we go through the examples later you'll see how the people need all their numbers.

Our outer personality cloak reflects either an involutionary or evolutionary quality. This is the main quality which will enable our soul to do the job it's chosen for this incarnation. However, it won't be able to do it as well as it might if we don't integrate all the numbers in our chart. Our incarnation has a particular overall colour, flavour. Then there is the shadow-part of that which defines us by giving us edges. One might say we begin, before incarnation, as a point. We then break down, refract, through our numbers, into colour and form which can be seen in the everyday world, others can respond and/or react to it/us, we can relate. Through our relationships we grow, and not only us but the earth grows with us through the matter our soul has borrowed to make our personality body. The soul knows about shadow, and uses it. Like painters, to help our soul do its job we must learn how to use shadow. We become Artists of Self.

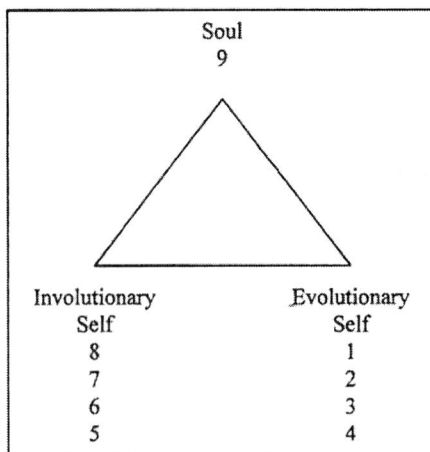

```
                        Soul
                         9




           Involutionary        Evolutionary
               Self                 Self
                8                    1
                7                    2
                6                    3
                5                    4
```

4

The Number Pairs

Now you have the basic patterns which the numbers make we go on to talk about the numbers themselves and how they work together in their pairs.

8 & 1 Infinity and the Ridgepole

8	1
Circle	Circle
Infinity	Ridgepole
Ancestors	Ego/Sensory-self
Spirit	Matter/Earth

8-ness: Infinity

8 is about the Ancestors. Get paper and pen and spend some time drawing 8s, Get the feel into your hand, arm, body. 8, like all numbers, is more than an intellectual exercise.

As you draw your 8 your pen flows round one circle, crosses over and flows round the other. You probably began your first circle going widdershins, got half way through it and turned deosil to do the bottom circle. You then crossed back over and went widdershins again to complete the top one. If you continue your pen going round and round over the 8 you find yourself travelling first one way and then the other. The figure 8 is one of the simplest spiral mazes which goes in both directions. This property of 8-ness is fundamental in how it works with spirit.

Ancestors are part of soul-groups, they're not always (or even often) DNA/blood/flesh and bone relations. The physical matter is not really crucial, except for the particular incarnation, to our purpose. The soul family to which we belong is far more significant. Sometimes our ancestors have shared family, racial and/or tribal lives with us but this is not a requirement. Souls experience all races and genders to complete their knowing of Life so blood-relations are a very small part of this. Our family, in soul terms, is our soul-group.

Ancestors hold the Cauldron of Memory, they are like the idea of potential in quantum physics or the akashic records in eastern traditions. They hold everything that is, was and will be. Sometimes this is called Spirit.

In Celtic lore Taliesin carries this energy, it is the energy of the one who knows all things. Robert Graves' translation of the Song of Amergin (Taliesin's Irish name) gives an idea of what this means ...

I am a stag of seven tines
I am a flood across a plain
I am a wind on a deep lake
I am a tear the Sun has let fall
I am a hawk above the cliff
I am a thorn beneath the nail
I am a wonder among flowers
I am a wizard, who but I
Sets the cool head aflame with smoke?

I am a spear that roars for blood
I am a salmon in a pool
I am a lure from paradise

42

I am a hill where poets walk
I am a boar ruthless and red
I am a breaker threatening doom
I am a tide that drags to death
I am an infant, who but I
Peeps from the unhewn dolmen arch?

I am the womb of every holt
I am the blaze on every hill
I am the queen of every hive
I am the shield for every hand
I am the tomb of every hope

This poem, and the Welsh story of Taliesin from the Mabinogion, give the idea of *knowing-through-being* all things. Taliesin/Amergin knows all these things because he is them, while at the same time retaining his consciousness of himself. This is very different to knowing about them, from study or reading or such. Taliesin/Amergin *knows in his bones* how it is to be a stag or a spear, a wind or a tear dropped by the Sun. At the same time, he might not know anything, academically, *about* these things.

It's a riddle poem. Riddle and satire were how the Celts transmitted knowing and knowledge, similar to the koans of Zen. Once one sees what they are saying the "aha" moment happens, there are no words to describe it. Ancestral knowing is like this.

Like all numbers, there are extremes which cause the person to go out of harmony, out of right relation with the world in which they live. To work well with your numbers you have to balance yourself between these extremes. It's like walking a tightrope and is often called 'the razor-edged path' in eso-speak.

The soul is the being that initiated this incarnation which you experience through your personality. The soul is part of a group, a family, a clan, of souls who are all working along similar lines to aid the growth of the overall Plan. This family, your family, will be found in the realm of the ancestors. The outer effect for you, as a personality, can be that you feel closer to some of your friends than your blood relations. Blood may be thicker than water but soul-links are far stronger than blood ties and they are much older.

Your soul came into being as part of a soul-group in what would seem a very long time ago to your personality, with its linear time-line. The soul has incarnated many times, into many forms, of both genders, all races, creeds and political persuasions. In some incarnations you've been quite a nasty person – we all have – in others you've been relatively nice. Sometimes you've been very clever, sometimes intelligent, sometimes dumb, sometimes you've been cruel, sometimes kind.

Your soul needs experience of all life-forms, all natures ... why? Because all of this goes into the Cauldron which is the universe, cosmos, god if you like. This Being, Intelligence, is continuously growing – through us, and through everything else in creation, trees, cats, cars, earthquakes, stars, computers. Every thing, from atom to star, is a means whereby this Intelligence can experience and grow.

The soul is a part of this Being, everything is. It is also conscious, aware, able to choose. Because of this consciousness it is able to make new experience so nothing is ever fixed.

The Ancestors hold the Thread of this idea. We can contact this energy, the thread of our soul-group by making conscious contact through our personality. The ancestors wait for us to come, they don't force themselves on us. We choose to go to their realm when we feel the urge, the itch, to explore what is beyond our personal world. Full understanding takes a lot of lifetimes but that's not a problem, imagine the adventures which lie before you-the-soul in future lifetimes. Exciting!

What are the extremes for 8-people?

It's very easy, as you may have found in your drawing, to get hypnotised into just flowing round and round the spiral. You don't want to stop, it feels so good. Now, take this idea into life … it could be a 'go with the flow' thing taken to extremes, so you flow so much you lose all identity, all individuation, go hither and yon without direction, losing the ability to concentrate and focus. This is no good at all for your soul. It has real difficulty inhabiting a gossamer-cobweb person. There's no security, no grail-cauldron for it to express itself through, no vehicle in which to do its work. Like grabbing at clouds.

So 8-people have to take care that, while they do go with the flow, they also have edges and boundaries, know self from not-self, are distinct enough not to invade other people's space. They have to be able, over their lifetime, to form their personality into a solid and useful grail-cup in which their soul can live and work. This is, after all, part of the bargain they made before they came into incarnation this time.

Another extreme 8-people can go to is a form of rigidity. They walk their spiral, but they tread so religiously in their own footsteps that eventually they find themselves treading a deep, narrow rut, always the same, no change, no growth, no evolution. This is very hard and difficult to climb out of. Imagine to yourself how it feels to be walking in a track just the width of your footsteps and perhaps so deep you can no longer see over the top. How could you climb out? And your view of the rest of the world would be severely limited, comprising largely of a strip of sky, perhaps some feet and ankles when other people came close to the edge of your rut. You've probably got the picture ... explore the analogies in terms of everyday life and relationships.

A simple one might be the way you drive or walk to work. Maybe you always take the same route. This can be very comforting and reassuring, you can listen to the radio, you don't have to think, you go on auto pilot ...

Now ... is this *always* a good thing?
Maybe you need a change, see something different, feel your brain firing at full capacity again and enjoying it. While routine is good, and useful, and pleasant it can become a treadmill which excludes growth. Again, our souls won't thank us for this. We'll also be rather dull and boring companions for our friends and loved ones – not surprising if they forget our birthday, or up and leave, perhaps!

So how does it feel to be at the point of balance for 8?
8 is on the *centripetal* involutionary cycle, working inwards and downwards. It is the number of Spirit, so it's about 'inspiriting matter', bringing heaven down to earth, which is one of the functions of being human.

It is also the number of the Ancestors, giving us a connection to the Ancestral Realm. The ancestors have great wisdom for us if we can contact them, including advice on how *not* to do things, how not to re-make the mistakes of the past.

Being on the widdershins spiral (1's spiral goes deosil), 8 is on the involutionary cycle, a time of in-breathing for the planet, which happens from midnight to midday. Inbreathing brings sky energy down into the Earth, an inseminating process-cycle, enlivening, quickening, the life-spark generating in the seed.

Both 8 and 1 work with forces which generate life.

So how does this apply to you?

As an 8-person, you elected, before you were conceived and along with your soul group, to do these same jobs of enlivening and quickening *in your own way* during your current lifetime. So your soul-job will be about ...

• Bringing heaven down to earth
• Enlivening Matter
• Inspiriting Matter
• Enabling seeds to spark to life
• Guarding entrances and crossroads

Hmm! you say, sounds like living in a fairytale! Well, stretch your imagination and think about real-life jobs and ways of living which do these things. Here's a short list of possibilities to get you going.

• Teacher, vocational trainer
• Gardener
• Farmer
• Sculptor/artist of any persuasion
• Computer programmer/designer, software writer
• Mother/father
• Business person
• Policeman

Quite a varied list? Now spend a little time getting your head around *how* each of the above do 8-work. Do a mind-map – yours won't be like this but the picture gives you an idea. Don't be neat, draw lines connecting everything that connects.

Then take your current job and do a mind-map to see how much 8-ness you already do. You may find it's quite a lot but you just hadn't noticed. Bringing it to consciousness is a primal step on the road to fulfilling your Self and your life through your number energy.

Remember, no one person ever has all the answers, so don't treat any book (including this one!) as *the* definitive lore. Each of us gives what we can at the time we write. Albert Newton said of himself that he was just a pebble on the sea-shore and, out there, is the vast ocean. If he, genius that he was, was a pebble then the rest of us might be grains of sand ... but, we're all necessary, including you.

1-ness: Ridgepole
1 is the partner of 8. As you've already seen, each of the pairs of numbers adds down to 9, the number of the Void, of potential, of enabling power. So, if you are an 8-person you also need to work with the 1, and if you are a 1-person you need to work with the 8.

The other half of your number pair will be your shadow side – in Ursula le Guinn's terms it will be the part which defines you, makes you visible as you. Shadows are what makes it possible to see, to define, to know where you are. You need your shadow or you could end up like Peter Pan.

As with 8, get paper and pen and give yourself some time drawing 1. Draw the 1 as a straight line, without the little flip at the top, this way you'll get the feeling of 'line', as you did with the floating curve of 8. Let the feeling flow into your body through your hand and arm. Don't try to translate the feeling, just experience it for the moment. Later, having fuelled up your Cauldron of the Unconscious, you'll be able to eat of the idea-soup it will contain. But, like all cooking, you have to let it brew … and a watched pot never boils! Even the unconscious works this way, so let it happen and don't try to explain it to yourself (and definitely not to anyone else). Give it time to develop into a juicy, nourishing broth, then you can really feast on it.

1 is the Ridgepole. In Taoist philosophy it holds up heaven, standing firm on the earth. 1 keeps heaven and earth apart, distinct, separate. It's like the original word, the Logos, which defined the pairs of opposites and made our universe possible.

So 1 has a very important *divisive* function. In spiritual work we're sometimes told that divisiveness is 'wrong'. This is a somewhat simplistic notion as it leaves out all the important material about boundaries, edges, self/not-self, and individuation, without which we cannot be properly functioning human beings.

1 is a number of discernment, knowing one thing from another, and without this faculty we wouldn't be able to know our ass from our elbow as the ancient adage goes. As 1 is about the body, Matter and the earth this doesn't seem too inappropriate.

1 is about knowing *self* from *other*. Differentiation is essential to knowing and, without knowing, we can easily become

'head-sets', full of knowledge which we splurge out inapprop-
riately swamping our hearers. 'Blind them with science' is
another old adage. Knowing when to speak and when to be
silent, how much/little to say, is a hallmark of the fully aware
1-person. It does usually take a bit of practice and making a
few mistakes to get to this point – that's OK, it's very likely
the sun will continue to rise each morning in spite of our
mistakes. A comforting thought, but not a reason for being
thoughtless and hedonistic, which are downside traits for 1-
people.

When you were drawing 1s you will have felt the up-down,
rocking, pendulum motion of the figure. It's a journey between
two points. Polarities. If you draw up and down over the same
line it's quite hypnotic, probably boring, and makes a hole in
the paper. Think about that.

What are these extremes for 1-people?
It's very possible to get stuck, to lose breadth of vision,
become myopic. All you can see is those two points, and the
only journey there is goes between them. A 1-person who has
got into this state can be quite aggressive to anyone who
suggests there might be another way. The 8 has its 'stuck in a
groove', so does the 1. They feel very different for the person
who is experiencing them but, to an outside observer, the
'stuck-ness' is both obvious and similar.

1-people, because of their strong heaven/earth polarity, can be
quite difficult to coax out of their rut. Helpers have to learn to
duck fast as 1-people can lash out like lightning, so fancy
footwork is a good idea for those who would like to help, and
1-people are very worthwhile helping. They are towers of
strength, the figure 1 is a tower-like image. They can be
swords to fight battles, often for others than themselves and
for causes which they espouse. Where these causes are
evolutionary, such as environmental campaigns, education,

stopping cruelty, greed and poverty, for instance – the 1-person can be an exceptional leader.

Leadership is a fundamental trait of 1-ness. Up-front and out there, 1-people do this very well. What they, and the world, need is for them to have a handle on discrimination *before* they rush to sort the world out.

1-ness is also about beginnings. 1-people initiate things. They also have to learn to complete them, a function of the line which goes *all the way* between two points.

So the basic extremes for 1-people are stuck-ness, getting in a rut, narrow vision and pushing everyone else along with their idea of right. These are qualities of a self-image which has become distorted through introspection. 1-people are also excellent naval-gazers, they can become so singular that, to quote an excellent Harrison Ford film, they feel *'Everyone's lost but me!'*. With loving help 1-people can be persuaded to climb out of this pit.

So how does it feel to be at the point of balance for 1?

Poised is the word which springs to mind. It's like the grace and balance of a tight-rope walker (remember that image was used for 8-people, 1-people's shadow side). There's a picture of Blondin walking the tight-rope across Niagara Falls in the nineteenth century which gives the idea. Arthur Rackham too has a beautiful picture of fairies dancing along a strand of cobweb. Both give a sense of the balance possible.

1 is on the centrifugal function, the outward and upward spiral which is expansive. As partner to the 8 it is about expanding, growing, evolving. Both 8 and 1 make a circle pattern, as you've seen. The circle is about holding, defining, making apparent.

As a 1-person, your job this lifetime might be about ...

• Leading
• Inclusivity
• Change
• Expansion
• New beginnings

As with 8, expand your imagination to bring these ideas into everyday living. Some possible jobs might be ...

• Administrator/civil servant
• Architect
• Artist
• Politician
• Scientist/explorer
• Business person

Some of the jobs are similar to those suggested for the 8-person – as 1 and 8 are partners this is to be expected. But the 1-person will do them in a different way to the 8-person. Do some more mind-maps around each job and see what comes to you. Then, as a 1-person, mind-map your own current job and see how it relates to the job-qualities (not the actual jobs!) above. You are bringing all this to consciousness, your consciousness, and so making it real for yourself, which is what numerology (like all spiritual disciplines) is about.

To be a complete 8 or 1 person, a soul-infused personality, you need to integrate the qualities of both Infinity and the Ridgepole. One of them will be your outer personality

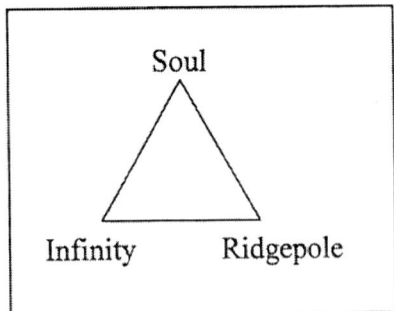

Soul

Infinity   Ridgepole

cloak, but that cloak needs its lining which is the shadow part. If you are an 8-person you will need the qualities of 1-ness to be whole and integrated.

If you are a 1-person you'll want to incorporate the qualities of 8-ness.

Wholeness is the quality we are striving for.

7 & 2   Love/Wisdom and Duality

7	2
Nonagon	Nonagon
Love/Wisdom	Emotions/Feelings
Inclusion	Separation
Flowing	Water

7-ness: Love/Wisdom

7 As before, begin getting to know 7-ness by drawing it.

NB – for this exercise, cross your sevens even if you don't normally do this, you'll see why when you come to explore 2.

You begin with a line going from left to right, then you dive down on a diagonal from right to left. Now your pen comes off the paper and back down again to draw a horizontal line across the downward diagonal. Drawing 7 has a rhythm, doesn't it? Thrum-da-da, thrum-da-da, a bit like a waltz.

7 is about Love/Wisdom. What is this?

It's easy to love foolishly and we all do it, it's a much more delicate process to love wisely. It's also very easy to be wise after the event, we all have 20/20 hindsight. Again it requires a lot of intelligent (not clever!) care and thought to be wise lovingly. When we have this little conundrum under our belts we are much more acceptable human beings than we were before.

What is love? Poets, essayists, novelists, film-makers, psychotherapists, singers and Uncle Tom Cobley and All have gone on about love for millennia. Lovers tend to get on with enjoying it and/or messing it up for themselves and everyone around them. Most of *us know* love when we see it or feel it, but how to say what it is?

EXERCISE: LOVE

When you feel love for a person, an animal, a place or whatever, what happens? What sensations come over you? Think about this now, just sit with the idea. Call to mind someone or somewhere you love dearly and allow yourself to experience the sensations which come as you do this. Don't try to control or analyse them, and certainly don't censor them. Jot down some brief word-pointers to remind you of the sensations after the exercise.

You may well find yourself 'going off', not seeing the everyday world but watching the person or place with your *mind's eye.* Allow this to happen. Come back to normality very gently as the experience wanes.

When you're ready, write some words in answer to the following questions. Don't try to make sense, be grammatical, spell correctly or write neatly, let go of all that and just put down the first words which come into your head.

• How did your body feel as you began?
• What sensations ran through your body as you brought the person/place to mind?
• Did your body shake? Tears, smile, other movement?
• Were you sexually aroused?
• Did you have sensations so intense as to be called exquisite?
• What sensations came as the image began to fade? [NB – you might feel *both* loss and relief at the same time.]
• How did your body feel after the experience was ended?

When you've jotted down responses to the stimuli-questions put your paper down, go and make yourself a hot drink. Then bring your drink, collect your piece of paper and go somewhere else, don't go back to the same physical environment in which you had the experience. Make sure it's somewhere you can curl up comfortably for a whole half-hour, on your own. Talking will wreck the whole experience, so don't … not however tempted you may be to splash your nearest and dearest with the marvellous revelations which have just come to you. Hold them secret, and sacred, for a while.

You have just had an experience of Love. *And* you've also found your own words to remind yourself of how it was. You've not had to take on my words (or anyone else's) which, while they fit me like a glove, are all the wrong shape and size for you. By the way, if nothing happened you obviously picked the wrong person or place. Try another.

Pain will have been one of the ingredients of your experience and this may surprise you. Pain is a part of love, without any need for sadism or masochism. Things can be so exquisitely beautiful they hurt. A painful time, perhaps a death or loss, can also be incredibly beautiful and full of joy … but it still hurts. If there is no pain then there is no real love, only emotional attachment and desire, 2-qualities not 7-ness. The pain of love is not that of a thwarted child but of an adult who is seeing and feeling far beyond themselves. This is what love is about.

What are the extremes of 7-ness?
One trait can be a propensity to drift off, to disappear into that glorious world of loving you just experienced and refuse to come back. A wish for the beauty of evolution without the work of involution, and 7 is the involutionary half of this pair. A number's down-side is often the up-side of its partner, as a master once said, *"Evil is inappropriate good"*, an idea worth pondering on. So, 7-people can wish to be gone from this world of tears. Those who trap themselves in fairyland in this way

often find it impossible to love in the real world. They may tell themselves, and everyone else, that this is right and proper and as it should be, that they are meant to love higher things. They have become so heavenly they're no earthly use!

Another trait can be to get addicted to these wonderful feelings and use anyone and everyone to get more of them.

A very subtle down-side is when the 7-person "gives everything away". At first glance, and certainly to themselves, this can seem like the ultimate act. However, a closer look shows it to be more like "spiritual anorexia", or sometimes bulimia. Both physical conditions often root into a person's feelings of unworthiness, undeserving, and there are usually similar roots for the spiritual condition.

Another down-side of 7-people is the need to be loved. This can come out as approval seeking, consequently the 7-person can be coerced into behaviour which is against their nature. It's a hard trait to get out of because it requires the person to risk losing love in order to be themselves, and this can seem to be a fate worse than death.

So how is it at the balance point for 7?

Very much a feeling of "this *and* that", the *and* / *and* principle. 7 is involutionary, on the centripetal, inward and downward spiral from heaven to earth, in-breathing, bringing Love-plus-Wisdom into earth-life, earth-knowing. It's about the intimate personal love *and* the expansive love for all creation, both at once. It's also about wisdom which knows *how* to love in each individual and unique situation.

Sometimes wise love requires us to stand back and allow disaster to happen so that learning can ensue. Sentimental-ism, and what might be called "motherliness and caring", must go out the window. It can appear cold and unfeeling to feeling-based people who are not yet come to wisdom, so it's a difficult and often misunderstood balance-point and, in consequence, can be hard to maintain.

The balanced Love/Wisdom person can also be the Consciousness Teacher. They learn from everyone they meet, books, TV, whatever, put all this in the mind-cauldron with the germ of a new idea, brew it, until it becomes a part of themselves. Then they can offer it to people and be heard. They are enchanters in the old sense. To en-chant is the practice of using the voice, words, to enfold the listeners in new thinking, new knowing, new seeing. The en-chanter, consciousness teacher, is one who has trained themselves, learned the deep meaning of language, the deep workings of the Earth and the elements. They are able to bring them all together, to portray the wholeness which they perceive in a manner which others can grasp. This is quite a feat – but it is within the ability of all of us if we choose to learn the skills.

7-ness is about …

- Sharing
- Love
- Allowing
- Letting go
- Being wise

Possible jobs might include …
- Doctor, nurse, therapist
- Farmer, gardener
- Parent
- Protestor, campaigner (e.g. Greenpeace, FOE, Oxfam)
- Teacher, particularly consciousness teacher
- Ecologist, vet

Mind-map these, feel into them and relate them to the 7 qualities above. If you are a 7-person, mind-map your own current job and see how it relates to the 7-ness qualities above. Some of the jobs, like parent, are done by people of all numbers but each of them will do the job differently. You might like to consider how each number does the job of parent and how each of these versions is useful. Of course, there are bad parents under every number but work on the idea of usefulness before you judge.

2-ness: Feelings/Emotions

2 is the partner of 7. As before, draw the figure 2 lots of times. See how similar the body-movements are to those you made when drawing the crossed 7. You begin with a line going from left to right, from the unconscious to the conscious. Then your pen goes down on the diagonal from right to left, from the conscious to the unconscious. Finally you make a horizontal line going from left to right again, from the unconscious to the conscious. These are the same movements that you made when you drew the crossed 7, except that you pen came off the paper to cross the 7 and it stays on the paper to make the bottom stroke of the 2.

The three moves, from unconscious to conscious, conscious to unconscious and finally unconscious to conscious again are significant. There's an old Zen adage which goes like this,

"In the beginning the trees are trees and the mountains are mountains. Then the trees are no longer trees and the mountains no longer mountains. Then the trees are trees again and the mountains are mountains."

This describes the process of the three strokes as we pass through the different aspects of the unconscious and the conscious. It is, strangely, and paradoxically, possible to be consciously unconscious, however it takes a while to achieve this so don't be in a rush. Glimmers of illumination sneak up on us if we just put the notion into our Cauldron of

Illumination (the Celtic initiation story of Taliesin is about this) and allow it to brew there until it (not we!) is ready.

2 is about duality, I and thou, polarity, both sides of the coin, the pairs of opposites. In 1-ness we explored this as the line which travels between two points, separation and individuation. Now, in 2, we explore a different facet, one which both discerns and integrates. When we work with 2-ness we see things as part of a whole *as well as* individual things in their own right.

2 is about the aspect of our personality body to do with water, Jung's feeling-function. It weaves between polarities enabling feelings to happen and to be expressed. Without the polarities there would be no feelings, we would be stuck, static, stationary, nowhere to move, nowhere to go. It is *movement* which is the medium of evolution. The e-motions, that which moves, are a power-house for change and growth. They are the spurs and lures which tease us out of our status quo. They get us to step out of our front door which, as Bilbo says, is a very dangerous thing to do. Once we set our foot on the road we can be swept off goodness knows where. We probably will be anyway if we are going to grow.

What extremes come up for 2-people?
Being led and ruled, by their feelings is the paramount one. The feeling function is very strong in all of us, even if we apparently suppress it. If you think about it, this suppression is also an *expression* of feelings we don't want to show.

2-people can come to believe it is the emotions, feelings, which hold the soul but this isn't the case. The soul sits balanced at the 3rd point between Love/Wisdom and Duality. However, there are many similarities between desire and love/wisdom which require us to use the wisdom-function to discern.

2-people can follow the lead of their feelings and allow their emotions to rule their lives, especially as we are much encouraged to "express our feelings" in the current world. Whilst it is good to do this, you do need to have acquired the discernment between expression and rule, without kidding yourself, in order to do it successfully.

Taking everything personally is another down-side of 2-ness and a root of the rages which stem from it. To take everything personally subtly inflates the ego until, usually without realising it, we become the centre of the world ... to ourselves. Anything which hurts us *must* have been directed to do so, the person intended our hurt. Extreme examples of out-of-control expression of feelings and taking everything personally are road-rage and other "tantrums" of over-exalted feelings.

In reality, the person who bumped into us in the supermarket queue probably didn't even notice us, and there's another subconscious grievance. They didn't even see us. This is a fear which lurks in back of the unconscious for the feeling-inflated 2-person ... "Perhaps I'm *not* the centre of the universe. Perhaps I'm so insignificant nobody notices me!". That can be a very hard one to bring to the surface and 2-people at the extreme of having feelings find ways to counter this by saying that "the other" is suppressing their feelings. This is a way of not accepting responsibility.

2-people share with 7-people the approval-seeking urge and the need to be loved. They usually come at it more aggressively than 7-people but the roots are similar. Both can feel insecure in their personalities and so reach outwards for love rather than inwards. To be loved means you are loveable, to be loveable you must love yourself. Both 2 and 7 people benefit from time alone, making friends with themselves, coming to accept both warts and good points. It can often be those good points which are hardest to accept and so a worse stumbling block than the warts. 2-people are often very good at knocking themselves down and lousy at appreciating their good points and this can easily make them dull, boring and aggressive ... and consequently not very loveable.

EXERCISE: GOOD & BAD POINTS

As an exercise, go and write down all your good points on one side of a page and all your bad points on the other, which is longer? Now, leave the piece of paper around where you can add to it over the next few days. Make a point of discovering more of the nice bits of you and writing them down. Grow that good-side list. Loveable people tend to be a balanced mix of good and bad. They are also comfortable with their bad bits and don't over-stress them by rejecting or trying to get rid of them. Neither works. What does work is to accept them without any great emphasis. One of my teachers used to tell me to take my bad bits and sit down together with them with a cup of coffee and a delicious Polish doughnut. "*After a little bit of enjoying yourselves,*" she would say, "*your horrid bit will come back to normal size.*" And she was right. Often I'd been making mountains out of molehills and felt quite inadequate to change ... don't we all?

So how is it to be balanced 2-person?

Here's a drawing of two different forms of balance. We can easily get into the first one and believe that's the only form of balance there is, two equal weights, equally spaced on each side of the fulcrum. But that isn't so. The second drawing is also balanced although the weight on the left is much larger than the weight on the right. It's very good for 2-people to expand their consciousness to encompass the balancing of unequal weights, it's a far more dynamic mode of being.

The weights don't have to be equal. What's important is that the weight times the distance on one side equals the weight times the distance on the other. Think about that – and translate it into everyday life situations.

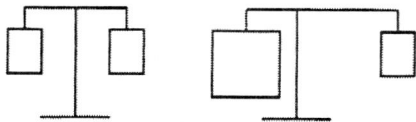

So, 2-ness is about ...
• Duality
• Feelings
• Pairs of opposites
• Two sides of one coin
• Conscious and unconscious
• Allowing the river to carry you and not needing to push it!

Possible jobs might include ...
• Mediator, lawyer
• Actor
• Administrator
• Shop-keeper
• Conservationist
• Translator
• Educator

Mind-map these, feel into them and relate them to the qualities above. If you are a 2-person, mind-map your current job and see how it relates to the qualities of 2-ness.

To be a complete 7 or 2 person, a soul-infused personality, you need to integrate the qualities of both Love/Wisdom and Duality. One of them will be your outer person-ality cloak but that cloak needs its lining which is the shadow part. If you are an 7-person you will need the qualities of 2-ness to be whole and integrated. If you are a 2-person you'll want to incorporate the qualities of 7-ness.

Wholeness is the quality we are striving for.

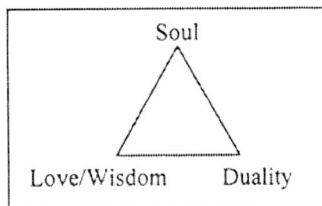

6 & 3   Knowing and Reason

6
Triangle
Knowing
See meaning
Communication

3
Triangle
Reason
Think logically
Air

6-ness: Knowing

Begin by drawing the figure 6. Feel that rhythm as your pen slides from the top right, round in a curve to the bottom where it curls up around and reverses to join itself at the middle. You make a half-moon, anti-clockwise and curve back on yourself to make a full circle at the bottom.

6 is about, gnosis, *knowing* ... what is this? Knowing involves the mind and the mental body which overlights the thinking function, intellect and reasoning, the 3-half of the pair.

If someone throws a bucket of water over you, you *know* you are wet. It has nothing to do with belief, thinking, there's no "perhaps" about it, it's nobody's opinion, you didn't need to go to evening classes or read it in a book. It's quite simple, you're wet! This sums up knowing, you can *know* anything in that same unarguable way even if you have no reasoning to justify it with. We all know things and often it's difficult to find words to describe our knowing, we use analogies, stories, like the one above. It's that flash where we are suddenly, and often inexplicably, certain of something.

6 is on the downward, centripetal, involutionary spiral. It's about bringing ideas down into matter which is sometimes called Active Intelligence in eso-speak. It enables the images and visions of spirit to be made real in this world. Without Mind to structure and shape their form the ideas and visions would waft about like lost ghosts. Many do just that because

there is no-one to give them a skeleton, through the Mind, on which the flesh of form can be woven by the 3-half of the pair.

So what about 6-people?
Wise owl is a good image and also holds some of the extreme-position difficulties common to 6-people. Owls are brilliant twilight and night hunters, they have fantastic night-vision and wonderfully precise hearing. They can pinpoint a mouse on the barn floor below by sound alone and then stoop straight onto it. Their wings are made so that they can fly silently. Owls often mate for life, although they may go off on their own in between bringing up their young.

Owls have been symbols of wisdom, and of death, in many traditions for millennia and many goddesses, such as Blodeuwedd who is a goddess of Spring in the Celtic tradition, have them as familiars. Florence Nightingale, who was a real force for change, had a Scops Owl who went everywhere with her, nesting in her pocket.

But most owls are not very awake and aware during the daylight, the Little Owl is an exception. Owls are not generally geared up for bright light and can become dazzled and confused by it. If Tawny Owls emerge during the day they are mobbed by other birds, even the little ones, like sparrows and tits, flock together and dive-bomb the poor owl until it goes back into hiding in it's tree-hole.

So it can be with 6-people. Mind, knowing, seeing the meaning in things, are not always acceptable in the bright light of everydayness. They tend to upturn established and comfortable apple-carts, which is not to most people's tastes.

The knowers have to know when knowing is going to be well received and when to keep their beaks shut. They also need to learn not to stuff it down everyone's throat, unasked for.

There's yet another old adage, now a motto of the SAS in Britain, *"To know, to dare, to be silent,"* which is well worth 6 people taking on board. The daring is often about that subtle form of risk, daring *not* to speak, which can be much harder than the risk of speaking. It's about daring to be silent, to allow people and things to take their own course, despite any knowing one might have of outcomes, learning to button up and not shoot their mouths off.

Additionally, knowing 6-people can have so much wisdom and information flowing through them that they talk the hind-legs off beachfulls of donkeys. This tends to put their audience off.

Active Intelligence is about knowing when to act and when to refrain from action.

6-people can lose touch with their 3-half, their shadow self, and fail to put a good structure on the information and knowing they wish to impart. As a consequence, their audience can feel as if they've been scatter-blasted with jello! Not constructive.

The wise owl can be the absent minded professor. Knowing can be filed in the Heap-System and, yes, the owl may know where everything is and they will undoubtedly affirm that they do, usually spluttering the while. But, when it comes down to it, they may need to investigate several heaps before happening on the right one.

There can also be a squirrel tendency, hoarding tons of dusty information, carting dozens of mouldy bags around, none of which has been used for aeons. Another thing squirrels do is to bury nuts all over the place then forget where they've buried them. For trees, this is really useful as it gets their seeds proliferated and builds new woodland as the forgotten nuts germinate and grow. This doesn't usually work quite as well for 6-people, they often end up with the equivalent of gardens full of the wrong sorts of trees, all crowded together so they don't grow properly and cut out all the light. The 6-person needs to take a machete to the lot in order to get some life back in the mental forest.

What is it like to be a balanced 6-person?

The other side of this is the awake and aware 6-person who grows a magical, enchanted forest, full of sunlit groves and a marvellous habitat for wildlife. This forest will have the right layering of tall, ancient trees, a mid-layer of faster growing and shorter-lived trees, and the bushes and plants of the bottom layer. Think about that habitat inside yourself.

Balanced 6-people work with the Mind, the magical mental energy which enables us to know things. It is the knowing which helps us to feel a part of everything, takes away the lonely feelings of separation that come of not being sure, not being certain, that we really are part of a whole. This knowing is about the connective, mental threads which everything (not just human beings) sends out so that it can be connected to everything else. We, humans, do this too – usually unconsciously – but we can learn to become conscious of the process. Discovering our own threads and their connections to everything else, brings a deeper level of knowing. Loneliness disappears, is a non sequitor because we are always connected to everything in background mode, but we are now conscious of it without it intruding on what we're focusing on at any time. 6-people are often closer to this realisation than others might be. They become beacons of this knowing consciousness for the rest of us to take light from.

6-people are about …

• Knowing
• Appropriate action
• Structuring ideas and visions

- Evoking knowing in others
- Giving voice to intuition

Possible jobs for 6-people might be ...

- Philosopher
- Shaman
- Statesman (not politician!)
- Mediator
- Teacher
- Writer

Mind-map these with the qualities above, get the feel of their relationships. If you are a 6-person, mind-map your own current job and see how it relates to the qualities of 6-ness.

Mind is fun and useful. The bad press is often caused by misconceptions of the qualities and purposes of Mind which do not take into account its divine creative nature. Wise owls *know* this.

3-ness: Reason
3 is the partner of 6. Draw the figure 3. Quite snaky, isn't it? The pen moves in a half-moon curve clockwise, and then does it again. It's got a sort of Vroom! Vroom! rhythm. Draw it lots of times and get the feel into your body.

The thinking-function, intellect and reason are qualities 3-ness enables in us. Without the thinking function we wouldn't be able to get up on time, do arithmetic or maths, drive the car, catch a train, do a shopping list, put our clothes on, all that semi-automatic stuff. And we wouldn't be able to see a good argument from a bad one, reason a case, see flaws and falsehoods. It is our thinking and memory which enable this, a very different thing from the *knowing* when someone is ly-ing to you to being able to prove it.

One of the things thinking is about is proof.

Thinking is very much the "god of our time". School and university encourage those to whom it comes easy, they can pass exams, get degrees. They also tend to function reasonably within the current rules of whatever society they live in whereas people who *know* can be very disruptive. Intuition (4-ness) and knowing-wisdom (6-ness) are not conducive to maintaining the status quo, 3-ness is much easier to control.

Thinking is a *function* of the mind rather than the quality of Mind which can readily see in a wise way. But it is thinking which will enable the person who has wisdom to formulate it in a way which others can see and/or hear.

We need reason, we shouldn't try to get rid of it but it's not good to make it a god either. Reason makes it possible to put ideas into words. The wise owl may be able to hoot but he or she needs a wider vocabulary than *Whoo! Whoo!* if non-owls are to understand them. Without the vocabulary the owl is likely to be mobbed ... as is the owl in the everyday world when he comes out of his hole in the daytime. With reason the owl is able to answer the questions which come in response to hearing his ideas and philosophies from those to whom they are new.

So what about 3-people?
3-people can easily get into the rut of thinking. Everything about them becomes heady, they won't do anything unless it's somehow proven to them ... often this "proof" is simply to see the thing in print or on TV, or said by someone with alphabet soup after their name. In this way the 3-person can lose all ability to reason. They completely forget all the things they know about seeing falsity and inconsistency and go haring off after the "fact" without "rhyme or reason". This can be very

irritating for those around them. It can also be dangerous. They will "follow the instructions" sometimes without taking the actual circumstances into account, they lose touch with reality. If they are in a life-saving situation, say, they could as easily kill as cure if they act only on knowledge without taking the real circumstances into account.

They may also be very unwilling to take risks, to go beyond the known, to climb out of their box, so giving themselves no opportunity to grow.

Descartes is quoted as saying, "*I think, therefore I am*". This has its good and bad points for 3-people. The power of the brain, of the synapses, is a vital part of being but it is not the *all* of being. As so often in life, and magical work, it isn't possible to answer everything from within only one discipline, within only one number, but 3-people can try to reduce it to this. On the other hand, 3-people can provide the engine which will enable the knowing-bus to go.

3-ness is about giving ideas form and shape and colour ... back to the torch exercise again. Without your hand between the light source and the wall, interrupting the flow of light and making shadows, you cannot see the colours of the light, nor its patterns. 3-ness is about this, about interrupting the flow and creating shadows which define things. The problem come when the 3-person begins to think the shadow is the reality rather than the form it has taken in order to be known.

Einstein told us that matter is highly compressed energy and this is a spiritual concept as well as one of physics. You might say matter is energy squeezed into form. The interruption of the light which creates colour and shadow is like this, it makes a form and shape for the light so that its various qualities can be seen. 3-ness is a way to do this. Reason is a means for clothing ideas in form so that they can be transmitted to others who haven't yet seen them or, at least, seen them in this particular way.

Being a head-set is another downside of 3-ness which you'll probably have already realised. They can probably explain away anything and talk the hind legs off a whole beachfull of donkeys, like their 6-partners but in a different way. They sound very reasonable too. If you're not good at this sort of thinking they will easily sidetrack you off what you know into believing you've got the whole thing round the back of your neck. You'll end up agreeing with them, thanking them, perhaps even being in awe of them ... then you'll get home and feel seriously confused because your body-knowing will be telling you everything your head has just got is *not* how it is at all. And they do this to themselves. It's a form of painting yourself into a corner, you get so hedged about with reasons and rules and conventions and regulations that you can't see straight. When it gets this bad the only way out is to cut the knot, crash the whole tower, like the Tower in the Tarot, knock down the edifice of thinking and start again. Many politicians and spin-doctors are head-sets.

What is it like to be a balanced 3-person?

Being balanced in 3-ness is a very *and/and* place. You have the intellect to know the whys and wherefores of things, how they work and how to mend them, where they are, what they do, when they are, who they are and why they are ... the basic questions of How, Where, What, When, Who and Why. Admittedly, the why-question is often very difficult and the best way to come at its answer is through the other five, but this too is something the balanced 3-person realises.

I said realises, meaning to make real, for themselves and others. This is a major 3-function, to make things real so that they can be seen and known by everyone. With the wise owl 6-person, they may know a lot but not be able to put it over. The 3-person may be able to put anything over, sell coal to

Newcastle as the old adage went, but not *know* a thing, only have the intellectual knowing about it, book-learning not body-knowing. The balanced 3-person is able to know what they don't know, know where to find someone who does know it and how to put that knowing together in a way which can be seen.

They're also good at reason. They can see inconsistencies, holes in theories, where someone hasn't been rigorous enough in their thinking. They may tend to say so-and-so has jumped to a conclusion in a derogatory way, perhaps because they don't yet have sufficient grasp of the knowing-principle of their intuition, but they can move past this. 3-ness isn't about intuition or direct knowing, gnosis, it's about giving this sometimes formless stuff a form. 3-people can in-form. They put a form on an idea and so it informs people. They give structure.

3-people are about ...

• Intellect
• Reason
• Thinking
• Structuring ideas and visions

Possible jobs for 3-people might be ...

• Science
• Metals
• Architecture
• Surgeon
• University lecturer
• And even politician ... hopefully one who thinks rather than spins.

To be a complete 6 or 3 person, a soul-infused personality, you need to integrate the qualities of both Knowing and Reason. One of them will be your outer personality cloak but that cloak needs its lining which is the shadow part. If you are an 6-person you will need the qualities of 3-ness to be whole and integrated. If you are a 3-person you'll want to incorporate the qualities of 6-ness.

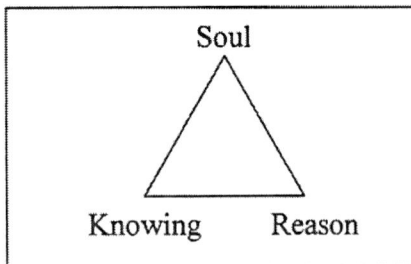

```
           Soul
            /\
           /  \
          /    \
         /_____\
     Knowing    Reason
```

Wholeness is the quality we are striving for.

5 & 4   Soul-Purpose and Intuition

5	4
Star	Star
Union	Connection
Soul-Purpose	Intuition

5-ness: Soul-Purpose

We'll begin by drawing the figure 5. People usually begin with the down-stroke, form the moon-curve and then take the pen off to put it back at the top and make the cross stroke. Do this several times ... da dee da, da dee da.

What is *soul-purpose?*

Soul-Purpose is the job the soul chose to do in this lifetime in concert with your soul-group, your soul-family. It is the reason why your soul incarnated this time around. The job it wants to do will be partly for its own growth but also to help in the overall plan of the universe. Usually we don't know what this is at first and maybe for quite a while in each lifetime, although a few people do, the Dali Lama is one of these along with some far less well-known people. Most of us get a case of spiritual amnesia at birth, and for good reasons. Not because we're "unworthy", stupid, bad or somehow "less" but because, if we retained the memory, it would influence the choices we make in ways which our soul knows wouldn't help in the sort of growth we need.

This might sound autocratic and overly parental but remember, the soul built our body and personality for the purposes of the soul-job. The personality which, while we're still unaware of our soul, seems to be "us" is only a part of the story and is certainly not the driver of our bus. There's an Arnold Schwarzenegger film, *Total Recall*, which gives an idea of this in a fun/fantasy story. The hero gets dreams and flashbacks of being another person. He gradually remembers more and more of "himself" then he sees an old video of himself talking to this person he now is, telling him that he is a "created personality", made for a particular purpose. In the film the purpose is evil and so is the "mastermind" who created the self he now is. He struggles against this and, of course, wins. He gains "total recall" of himself, all the memories which have made him who he is, and saves the planet in true Schwarzenegger style.

Your soul is not evil but the process of awakening to soul-purpose is often similar to that of the hero in the film. It may well begin with dreams, flashbacks, knowing a place you've never been to before, etc. If you follow these leads you uncover more and more of yourself. Some people resist, don't look, don't follow up. There's no compulsion from the soul to do so. However, if you do, life does open up enormously and become much more fun. People who know their soul-purpose, at least to some extent, are never bored.

Ursula le Guin, in Left hand of Darkness, says *"It's good to have an end to journey to, but it's the journey which matters in the end.* ". This is true. Life is a journey, the travels, adventures, difficulties, sorrows and joys are the meat of the journey. But it is good to have a destination to walk towards while taking one's time on the walk and observing every twist and turn of the way. Your soul-purpose is *both* that destination and the journey itself.

So, what are 5-people about?
They may well have spiritual amnesia but they will also have a pull, an itch, a knowing that the everyday life they lead is not all there is. They will always be hungry for meaning in life and this hunger is strong for them, stronger than for those whose number is not 5. There are other ways to come to soul-purpose besides being a 5-person but they will always,

somehow, involve 5-ness, perhaps through their name, or the name of the place where they live, or their house number. Even having a partner or a child whose number is 5, or with a 5-flavour, will initiate this. But those who have 5 as their birth number will have the urge very strongly. It's like the piece of grit in the oyster which irritates the animal so that it creates the pearl around the grit.

On the downside, 5-people with this itch can be difficult to live with. The itch will ride them and be more important than anything or anyone else. Partners will always be secondary to the discovery of the soul-purpose and to living it out. Two 5-people together can manage it as long as their egos don't try to bend each other to their own will. They can be selfish in their attitude and all goes down before their search for soul-purpose. There's no way their search is going to stop for anyone else but 5-people can learn to do their search without trampling everyone in the process.

Another downside trait is *"my Ox is THE Ox"* syndrome. This is an allusion to the Taoist story of the Ten Oxherding Pictures. In these, the boy who is searching for the Ox finds it and, at that point, believes it's THE OX, the only one in the universe and/or the only one worth having. 5-people can easily do this. Having found their path or, more likely, thinking they've found the path it's common to want everyone else to join it quite regardless of whether it's the path for them.

So 5-people have to learn to look at themselves with clear vision otherwise they can easily delude themselves. Finding one's soul-purpose is not necessarily easy. You can think you've got it, it looks good, fits your current box of what you think is right, so you gallop after it full tilt. 5-people need to keep their discrimination, or learn it if it's not one of the skills they brought with them this time. Objectivity can go out the window in the flush of excitement of glimpsing your soul-purpose.

So how is it to be a balanced 5-person?

Clear-headed certainty with a sense of humour which is able to laugh at oneself. A balanced 5-person will be able to stand back and get a perspective on their quest, see how their path might affect others and choose a way which will cause as little damage to others as possible. They will know not to hare off blindly without taking notice of everything in their path. This means all life, not just humans, and not just humans they care for. They will have a wider view on their place in the total scheme of things, being interested and concerned for all life on the whole planet and not only that which concerns themselves.

Because they know about the itch, the dream, the search for meaning, they can help others in the same boat. They will be able to speak out of themselves and not out of a book. As such, they will be authentic, consequently other soul-purpose seekers will be able to hear them successfully.

NB – being authentic is good for everyone. To speak out of one's own knowing is how to say useful things and all of us need to get to this place.

Seeking one's soul-purpose is not a selfish pursuit although it can begin that way. The beginner on this path may behave so but this is inexperience, like a child who doesn't yet know that they are not the centre of the universe. Once they have mastered this idea they can inspire others to the same end.

Jobs for soul-purpose seekers, 5-people, can be just about anything. What they do will be indicated by the stronger numbers in the rest of their chart. If they are fairly conversant with the 5-ness path they may well choose a job which involves talking to people. This could be as indirect as writing or journalism, or as direct being a counsellor, priest, financial adviser or social worker. The excitement of looking for and finding one's soul-purpose can light a fire within the self which encourages the 5-person to want to offer the same joy to others.

5-ness is both a difficult and a joyful path. It's a common one in people associated with "new age" and mind/body/spirit work for obvious reasons, but it's certainly not exclusive to the spiritual development lines. People look for and find their soul-purpose within any and all walks of life. The "my ox" syndrome must always be watched for, it is exclusive and soul-purpose is never this but always includes all paths and means, however strange these may appear at first.

Possible jobs for 5-people might be anything at all, as I said above. But, whatever it is, the 5-person will be on the search and able to help others with this too, once they realise themselves.

4-ness: Intuition and the Will
Draw the figure 4. It's a three-stage process, first a diagonal from top-right to bottom left, then a crossbar, then you take the pen off the paper and connect the top-right of the diagonal line vertically downwards through the crossbar and a short distance beyond, then stop. Da-da daaa, da-da daaa, there's a sort of in-breath hop after drawing the diagonal and crossbar while you lift the pen, move it and put it down again to do the final stroke. Draw 4 lots of times and get this hop-step-and-and-jump feel into yourself.

4-ness is about the intuition and also about the will which drives this process. In order to make the hop, step and jump to daring to use the intuition, your personal will needs to drive you on, get you to shut your eyes and jump, not knowing the outcome. In the 21st century we're not much encouraged to use our intuition, to develop our intuitive powers, the society we live in likes to have things proven to the intellect. This naturally limits what it is possible for people to know, to what fits inside the intellect-box ... and that's actually not a lot. Also, using the intuition isn't "safe". You may well not be able to use statistics to prove many things which you know actually happen, particularly those hunches which come off right and everyone tells you are "pure coincidence".

Let's look at the word *coincidence*, what does it mean? It comes from to *coincide* which means to be identical. A coincidence is when an event happens at the same time as another event without any *apparent* connection between them, apparent at least to logical thinking. It is similar to synchronicity.

The intuitive process is like this. Things happen without any apparent connection or immediate cause or, at least, a normal, physical cause. That can be scary if you're not accustomed to it and don't have an adventurous disposition. People who are intuitive often get criticised by those who are not using their intuitive powers and don't wish to.

4-people touch into their intuition and are not likely to be scared by it. They can be quite scary to those who don't though, especially as the will to be intuitive is strong in them. They don't want to suppress it, they want to use it, they see things very quickly, as a whole, without having to make the (to them) wearisome journey from *a-to-b-to-c* etc, as the more intellectual, linear thinker does.

Geniuses have a strong 4-ness in them although they are not necessarily 4-people. Just because you're a 4-person don't necessarily fool yourself into believing you're a second Einstein, you may be, but you may not too.

Using the intuition enables you to see the threads which connect things far more easily than you would through the intellect. Using the intellect is very hard work if you want to see the interconnectedness of things. Things don't connect in long, linear chains, they connect in three dimensional web-like patterns, wholenesses. Computers are intellectual things, they think in a linear fashion which is why they get apparently obvious (to us humans who don't naturally think in a linear way) things wrong, why they are hard for many people to understand. School, and sometimes university, education can tend to prefer the linear-thinking mode, again why a lot of people find it hard work. Inappropriate use of, and emphasis on, computers can encourage people to try to think like them ... with disastrous results. Brains do not function like computers!

This doesn't mean computers are "bad", just that they need to be used with common sense, like everything else, and not made into gods.

So, what are 4-people about?
They are intuitives. They see things without having to reason out how to do it. However, like 6-people, this can mean they have difficulty telling others about what they've seen, they need some 3-ness to help with this. 4-people are different from 6-people in that, when the 4-ness is strong, they *live in both worlds at once*, the normal everyday and Otherworld. 6-people don't do this, they *know* across the worlds, and without rhyme or reason sometimes, but they don't actually walk both worlds at once. They need 4-ness for this.

4-people are walkers between worlds. This is a difficult thing to be and can lead to forms of psychosis when the person is not trained, or experienced, in being in more than one place at once *and* retaining their individual identity. If you are a 4-person and feel the urge to journey, travel across the worlds, find yourself an experienced teacher ... not one who quotes rules! ... who can do this themselves and ask to be taught by them. Unfortunately, such teachers don't grow on every bush nor are there many of them to the pound. There are many teachers who would like to teach you ... beware of them. The teacher who *can* do it will do their utmost to talk you out of it, not answer the phone, tell you how bad it will be, suggest you don't bother, probably be quite rude. When you find one like this you have struck gold. They really do know the way, they really can go out and come home again, they really can rescue you if you get into trouble ... as you assuredly will on the path of intuition. Likely they will be another 4-person or have 4-ness strongly in their chart but, if you start to ask them about this they'll lead you up the garden path and back again. Good walkers between worlds are also rocket-science tricksters, it goes with the territory. They are also extremely good fun to be with, very compassionate, caring, honest and truthful.

Because they can see the interconnectedness of everything, at first hand, they will have equal compassion for a cat, a child, their car, a carrot, the planet and the tiniest microbe or particle of matter. It's impossible for them to be "humans first" people because to be such is a non sequitor for them. It makes no sense as they can see the life energy of everything, and see that it is the same even if in different form. They *know* that the matter which makes their own bodies is the same matter which makes up their car or a star, so how can they care more for one form than another, they will ask you.

This is a hard place to live in most societies. Most people care for humans first, before anything else. They feel separate from other life-forms, from the planet herself, from the stars. 4-people have to learn to live in this society, which will think them both stupid and crazy and so shun them, whilst still holding onto themselves, their 4-ness. They can become depressed and have psychological problems from trying to keep themselves hidden and hearing what is to them "crazy talk", from having to live outwardly as if they held the same mores as the people around them.

What is it like to be a balanced 4-person?
Light and laughter spring to mind. They will have a wicked sense of humour ... there's that trickster element again ... combined with a great compassion. What they need most in order to survive is a strong and integrated personality. Once they have this then they will be able to "fly" with both feet on the ground. This sounds like a paradox but think about it. The 4-person is wholly connected to earth and yet is able to walk in otherworld, they are a connector between the two.

They will probably need to work with something connected to the earth and possibly to people as well, perhaps in some sort of educating capacity or social work which will allow them the opportunity to example connectedness. They need to take care they don't proselytise for such teaching doesn't work. It may provide a bunch of acolytes and disciples but it won't give people the ability to see things for themselves. Disaffected disciples will turn on their previous master and rend them tooth and claw ... 4-people need to be aware of this. The balanced 4-person works, without becoming a guru, on the job of helping people to open their own eyes to reality. Teaching without teaching it's sometimes called.

4-people are good at reality, this is the 4-square aspect of themselves. They can be well earthed, grounded. They are not usually worried when reality doesn't look how it says in the book or seems frightening. Reality is the unknown. Their instinctual link gives them the bridge. They may seem unusual to others but they will have a warmth about them which carries people over the gulf of dissimilar thinking reasonably easily. Once they are balanced they become very attractive.

Possible jobs for 4-people might be ...

• Shaman
• Doctor

- Philosopher
- Writer
- Inventor
- Gardener, working with the land, ecology
- Scientist

To be a complete 5 or 4 person, a soul-infused personality, you need to integrate the qualities of both Soul-Purpose and Intuition. One of them will be your outer personality cloak but that cloak needs its lining which is the shadow part. If you are an 5-person you will need the qualities of 4-ness to be whole and integrated. If you are a 4-person you'll want to incorporate the qualities of 5-ness.

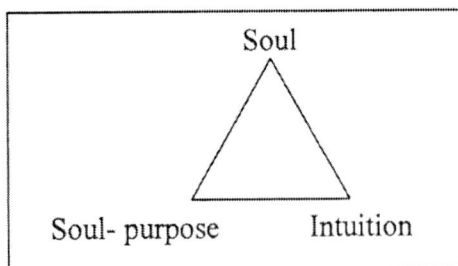

Wholeness is the quality we are striving for.

9 & 0   The Void and the Sun

9	0
Dot	Circle
Void	Sun
Chaos	Mirror
Invisible force	Container of force – Cauldron

9-ness: The Void

A major attribute of 9, as a number, is that once you've reached it you go up an order of magnitude, get larger by more than the sum of your parts. 9 is the stepping stone to another level, both arithmetically and spiritually. It also means that, having achieved a height you go back to the bottom of the ladder again ... but this is the next ladder.

9 is related to the king of the Underworld who, in many traditions, has *a cap of darkness* and a *cauldron* amongst his treasures. The cap of darkness is the cap of invisibility, one of nine's major attributes. One mythological wearer of this cap is Hermes, Mercury, the messenger and Trickster, god of communication, who symbolises the interconnectedness of the life threads through the flowing, liquid metal, quicksilver.

9 also has the power-qualities of a black hole. No light can escape from a black hole because of its immense gravitational field – another way of being invisible. It also has worm-hole qualities of communication across otherwise impossible boundaries, a dimension changing ability. 9 enables communication across the worlds, across the realms and kingdoms of nature as well as the stars, universes and spiritual kingdoms.

9 makes change happen. It is power, but not power over. 9 is the *power* to ... power to love, power to help, power to care. It's the will. Sometimes people call this the "will to *do* good" but this is not so. The "will to good" is not the same as doing good. Doing good can be one of the downsides of 9. It often means doing what you think is best and, usually, without asking the recipient if what you're going to do is of the least use to them or will only make things worse. The "will to good" is allowing, doesn't know best, it is open to outcomes it had never dreamed of ... a very different thing.

Draw a simple **9**. Your pen does two things, first it goes round in a widdershins circle then it goes downwards in a straight line. **9** is made of a circle and a line, it holds two ideas, both of which are never ending in their own ways.

When you draw it, you arbitrarily decide to begin and finish drawing a circle at a particular point. Similarly, you decide to begin and end a straight line. It could go on forever in both directions but it doesn't, it finishes, becomes complete, as does the circle part of the **9**. So, in drawing **9**, you are drawing two versions of eternity, circle and line, and combining them together ... an *and/and* concept. That says a lot about the qualities of **9**. Enabling power is inclusive, not separatist.

Spend some time drawing nines. Nine has a rhythm too, deeda, uneven, it has movement, as you stop you want to start again. We all write sloppily some of the time but there's something of an innate need to complete the figure nine. This too expresses 9-ness, it's a number of completion, the act of completion, and, at the same time, the will to begin again. This quality helps 9-people be good at manifesting.

This is the energy of no-thing-ness, the potential from which all things come. In Celtic lore several of the "dark gods" carry this energy, including Arawn, Beli and Gwynn, the Greeks called it Hades, the Romans Pluto.

Its name, the Void, Chaos, can feel scary. Chaos, as an idea, has a very bad press, usually because it threatens all of the structures which we have become accustomed to. We fear it because it is likely to pull our lives apart so that we lose everything.

As most human beings, most creatures perhaps, build their reality on "things" the idea of chaos sounds like the end of the world. In a sense, of course, it is. It's the end of the reality we've become accustomed to. But it certainly isn't the end of reality.

We've talked about human beings dislike of change. This fear and dislike is usually the root of the ills which befall us, individually and as a species. However, knowing that doesn't usually make change any more palatable.

The energy of 9 causes change. It's the power of chaos behind the Big Bang theory, it's the power of Black Holes, of supernova. It breaks up stagnant order, puts all the primal material into the melting pot, so that new order can emerge. It's the power of Butterfly Soup. As Richard Bach says, in Illusions, "*What the caterpillar calls a nervous breakdown the master calls a butterfly.*"

The transformation of the caterpillar into the butterfly is, perhaps, the best known and most staggering of nature's miracles, and one we can watch each year. Caterpillars eat and gorge themselves all summer, shedding skin after skin, until autumn. Then a purpose drives them to find a safe place, to spin silk out of their guts and build themselves a chrysalis, a cauldron, an alchemical flask. They build this chrysalis-flask around themselves. When it is done they are entombed, or is that enwombed, within it and an incredible transformation begins. The caterpillar dissolves down into its component atoms, and then all those atoms come back together in a new form ... the butterfly. How does that happen? What is it that *knows* how to rebuild the form and what shape to rebuild it into? Science cannot answer that as yet. It says the innate pattern is in the genes which pulls it all together in the new form, but where has this come from?

There is much discussion about consciousness in science, philosophy, religious and esoteric circles. Sometimes they even all get together to trade ideas. They seem to get closer and closer to the ancient realisation that consciousness is a power which shapes reality. 9 is about this, about the power which knows how to dissolve a caterpillar's body and reform it as a butterfly.

As with all the rays, we can contact and interact with this energy, this power. It can inform our lives. But, to work with it, we must grow beyond the fear of change which makes us do all we can to stay the same. There is, as far as anyone knows, always the fear of change but this fear doesn't have to grow into the beast which blocks change. Fear of the unknown is normal , part of the thrill. Fear of fear, fear which petrifies (turns to stone) is no good and will kill the person who has it. It will turn them to stone in ways which will choke out their lives. They will become mentally and physically stuck, unable to move, and this kind of stagnation affects all parts of the body and mind.

The chaos energy of 9 breaks up this crystallisation, petrification, stagnation. It can appear violent and rough to us, from our personal perspective. It's a huge step forward for each of us to find ourselves at a place where we can contemplate this sort of change without shutting down. Once we can, we are able to work with this energy. Our lives become far more exciting and alive – and we are able to be more useful in the world. Once we begin to wish to be of use in the world and not just to ourselves, the energy can work with us.

It's necessary that we have taken the mental step out of selfishness before 9 energy can become conscious within us. Chaos is inclusive, life-promoting, life- enhancing. We have to change, to grow out of the hand-me-down perspectives that change is bad before it can become conscious within us.

EXERCISE – 9 & 0

9 and 0 are expressed as a pair in the glyph of the sun, ☉. Here is an exercise which will help you get the feel of the powers which express themselves through these numbers.

Sit or lie quietly. Become aware of your breathing. Don't try to change anything, just hear and feel the movement of air into and out of your body, your lungs, as they suck air in and blow it out again.

The rhythm is hypnotic and you may find it slows down as you become accustomed to it. Allow the rhythm to transport you.

You are out in space, in the velvety blackness surrounded by a myriad of beautiful stars, like diamonds on velvet. Feel yourself to be a point of light, like a star. Feel yourself becoming infinitely small and yet you're always there. The smaller you become the more intense your sense of being and self.

Now, allow yourself to expand. You become bigger and bigger until you encompass the whole universe. Your sense of beingness is now as fine as gossamer and yet it is still strong as steel. Again, the larger you become the more intense your sense of being yourself.

Contract again, become a pinpoint of light. Expand again and become the whole universe. Spend a little time moving between these two states.

Come to a place of stillness, try holding both concepts within you, so you are both infinitely small and infinitely huge at the same time. You are both, and one. You are a point of light within a greater light.

Be still there. Allow the sensations to flow through you.

Don't try to analyse, just BE.
When you are ready, allow yourself to come back to body-consciousness. Bring yourself back from space, come back to earth, your home. Feel yourself within your physical body again. Become aware of your breathing, follow its rhythm but, this time, allow it to bring you back to your body.

As you become aware of your body again you may find it actually feels big. This is OK. You are in fact physically sensing your etheric body which, normally, you are unaware of. It is bigger than your physical body, so you are sensing reality. Don't worry, begin to move your fingers and toes. At first it might seem a bit difficult, just keep on doing it. Gradually your awareness will return to its usual state where you are primarily conscious of your physical body. But, now you've *consciously* known the feel of your etheric body, you will be able to do it again.

What happened in the exercise?

You *became* the *glyph,* the ⊙, the dot within the circle. You knew yourself to be a point of light within a greater light. You now have a sense, a body-knowing, of the combined energies of the nine and the zero. The nine is the dot, the zero is the circle.

You now have a sense of that intense power which is 9-ness. And you have a sense of that gossamer tenuous strength and light which encompasses all things, the energy of the zero.

These two numbers hold the power of creation.

So what are 9-people about?

In the examples chapter there's a 9-person, Anny. Looking at her numbers will tell you a lot, but there are as many variations on that as there are 9-people.

9-people are manifestors, they make things happen. Also radical changes happen around them. They can appear magical and superhuman. On the downside, this can be intimidating for those in their vicinity, so 9-people have to learn to keep their cloak of invisibility and illusion around them so that others are comfortable. And they can slip into the place of "power over" with dreadful consequences.

As I've said, 9 is the power which drives the engines of other numbers, so what 9-people are like and how they work will depend on the other numbers in their chart. Anny has a strong intuitive aspect, her 9s drive this. With her name number she gets a very strong sense of soul-purpose and, again, her 9s drive that too. But if your overall number, either birth or name, is 9 then you will be a driving force, a catalyst for change in whatever you do.

For you, as a 9-person, this probably won't be excessively uncomfortable but those who ride the changes with you may not feel so sanguine about it. 9-people don't usually mind change too much, they even enjoy it, at least some of the time. This doesn't necessarily mean they are rootless, eternal travellers, unable to commit themselves to anything, probably just the opposite. The power of 9 is also about purpose, it's not a feckless thing, and it is this sense of purpose which can intimidate those around them. This isn't necessarily the same as the soul-purpose. 9-people can channel change for evil as well as change for good, whatever they do will be very difficult to withstand.

If there is a strong 1-energy the 9-person is likely to be a great leader. Whatever cause they espouse will prosper. If the 1-energy isn't so strong then they will lead from behind the scenes, empowering others to be the focus of their purpose rather than heading it up themselves.

Whatever, their passion will be very strong. They will probably also have a form of charisma which will cause others to want to follow them. If they have a strong intuitive side as well then they will appear uncanny in the way they know things, able to read your mind.

But they are not necessarily a power for evil. They are just a power and how that power comes to be used will depend on the rest of the numbers in their birth and name charts. It's those which give the pointers to how the power is used.

What is it like to be a balanced 9-person?
No, this isn't a contradiction in terms. The balanced 9-person will have done a tremendous amount of work on themselves, they will have an integrated personality which will not be phased by any one of the subtle bodies/functions. They won't stuff their emotions nor will they let them ride roughshod over everyone. They won't be stuck in their heads but they will be able to think clearly and see connections fast. They will honour and enjoy their bodies but not in a licentious way, and they will have a good handle on both instinct and intuition as well as their soul purpose.

They will probably seem both old and young at the same time. They may also appear distant, you may find it hard to know them or get close. 9 is the invisible power, those who work from here will not be easy to see, much of themselves will remain invisible unless you know how to look. They will probably get on well with 5 and 4 people, there is a lot of similarity even though differently arrived at.

As far as jobs go, they are similar to 5-people. Whatever they do will depend on the rest of their numbers spread, and they could do anything. They are difficult to know but those who work at it often say it was worth the effort.

Zero-ness: The Sun

Zero is about no-thing-ness but at the other end of the scale from 9.

As you've seen, if you do the zero-times table you end up with nothing. Zero is about the inexpressible, eternity and continuity. We don't end when our current body dies. If you consider it biologically every cell in your body has died and been replaced, some many times, by the time you are seven years old. But you remain.

This process of dying cells and replacements continues all your life. When you hoover up the dust quite a lot of that dust is your own cells. But *you* still remain. If anything, your personality gets larger and hopefully more inclusive. So ... the cells of your body are *not* the essential you.

As you saw, 0+0=0. This is a weird thing to get your head around. Intellectually, at first, it feels as though you can just brush it off with "Well, of course! So what?". But the concept nags at you, turns up at odd moments and presents itself for viewing.

Zero holds the essence of things, in this way it is no-thing itself but it is the essence of Life, that which inspirits. It is also the web which connects all things.

On 3rd March 2004 the Rosetta comet-intercept spacecraft was launched for a ten year voyage to the comet Churyumov-Gerasimenko. It's hoped to put a lander on the comet and take samples of its matter. The scientists hope that this data will provide new insights into the origin of life. They believe that all the atoms of our body are "stardust", to quote the 1960s singer Joni Mitchell, and the structure of the comet has the atoms which were there at the Big Bang. So the cellular and atomic knowing of the matter of our bodies has the memory within it of everything back to the Big Bang (and possibly before but that's not a scientific statement), it does indeed know all things.

Science also knows there is some means by which a particle on one side of the universe knows what is happening to a sister particle on the other side of the universe. A change which happens in one simultaneously happens in the other. They can't yet explain how this works but they know it does. Again this seems similar to Taliesin's knowing of all things in that he, too, instantly knows of all things because of his conscious connection with all life.

Zero connects through being-ness, it's like a cosmic internet, a cosmic web to which we can all attune. It requires training to do so, we have to be very well aware of ourselves in order to be well aware of the universe. We must see clearly and not be befogged by wishful thinking. Zero energy helps with this. It acts as a mirror, reflecting everything back to itself, to whatever its light touches. When you begin to work with zero energy it can be dazzling because it collects all the light of whatever is before it and reflects it back. At first, this is so bright we see nothing, only the light. If we choose to learn then we stay with the experience and, gradually, become accustomed to the light. If you've been to a symphony concert the effect is similar. When you first go pretty well all you hear is sound. As you continue to go your ear learns to distinguish the parts of the orchestra, the different tunes and rhythms which combine to make the whole. So it is with the mirror-bright light of zero, except what you come to see is the various rhythms and tunes and colours which make up yourself.

As you get to know yourself this way so your vision expands, you are able to realise that you are a microcosmic version of the whole, you are the universe in little. As you come to know this so you realise that to make the world more whole you work first on yourself, the little part of the universe which is you. Everyone doing this means the universe becomes whole, piece by piece.

The zero holds the energies of the sun, our personal star here on Planet Earth. The sun is the light-bringer, energy and life giver. Without the sun we wouldn't exist.

The sun is also a wonderful maelstrom of enormous energies. It's a nuclear fusion bomb continually going off – NOTE, *fusion* not fission! Fusion is the bringing together of things, fission is blowing them apart. This is very significant. The sun is about bringing together, one of the functions of love. It is through this function that it enables life to *be*.

The sun gives light, which enables us to see, both physically and etherically, so we can see the visible wart on our friend's nose *and* the etheric wart on their personality. This can be uncomfortable for all parties and is a trait to be used with great compassion. Don't shoot your mouth off just because you can see a hole in someone's shoe, or in their personality.

People with zeros are mirrors. They reflect back what they see, another uncomfortable trait. Sometimes their mirror is too bright, too clear, and so blinds the person it is reflecting, which is disabling, one of the down-sides of the zero.

Zero-people love completeness.

They are *containers* for power – cauldrons.

Draw a zero. Draw lots of zeros. Get the feel of zero into your body. What happens to you as you draw this figure?

The circular path is one which human beings naturally wish to follow. There is a strong "there and back again" feel to it, like Bilbo's journey in The Hobbit, and Bilbo is very happy to return, to come home. He is less happy that home isn't quite the same as it was before he went.

There are lots of adages from around the world which express this such as *"You can't step into the same river twice"*. Ursula Le Guinn expresses it very well in her novel *The Dispossessed* ...

You can go home again, the General Temporal Theory asserts, so long as you understand that home is a place you have never yet been.

On the spiral path home is different ... and yet more the same. You land on another turn from where home was on the previous spiral, you have a different perspective on it, one of distance in time. This distance in time actually gives you more 'space' in which to be. You don't have to try and go back to being the person you were when you left home, which is impossible anyway, you can be the enlarged person your travels have helped you become. So home is the same *and* different, but it is not a place you have ever been before.

The zero becomes a spiral. Try drawing this in the air now, not on paper, allowing your hand to rise with each turn. How does this feel?

Our ancestors understood the significance of the spiral, for instance it is one of the fundamental designs in Celtic art dating back many thousands of years. Perhaps one of the most typical is the three-pronged spiral or triskele, more elaborate spirals are based on this fundamental pattern. The number three was of deep significance in many traditions. Here is an example of the triskele form. Try following the spiral round with your finger, what does your body feel? It seems our Celtic ancestors certainly knew a thing or two about involution and evolution as the spiral is a fundamental part of their art.

Of course, there are no zero-people, nobody has zero as their number. Even more than 9, zero is not of this world in a physical sense but, without it, nothing can be.

5

Working with your Numbers

Your birth number, the number all the figures in your date of birth reduce down to, is your major trait for this incarnation. This is the "job description" you agreed to, with your soul group, before you came into incarnation this time. You need to explore this number in depth and I give you some exercises to do this.

In order to do your soul-job well you need to come to a real understanding of just what it is you took on – just as you do in doing your everyday job. This process can take years and you will always be seeing new bits, new insights. It's like watching a really good film, or reading an excellent book, one which you can see or read over and over again. Each time, you see a little bit more, something new, get a new angle on it. You life is a bit like Doctor Who's spaceship, the Tardis, much bigger inside than it appears on the outside. Your life is an excellent story, well worth exploring and the numbers offer you pathways to do this.

Calculations

Calculating your numbers with this system is very simple and, like most numerology systems, is one of reduction – i.e.

$$23 = 2+3 = 5$$

Birth Number

Your birth number was arranged and calculated by you-the-soul in concert with your soul-group/clan before your were conceived. You can't change this number – so you organise your other numbers to work with it, in support of your job for this lifetime.

Your birth number is composed of

•DAY – relationship of the earth to herself, twenty-four hour period in which you were actually born, one rotation of the Earth on its axis.

• MONTH – relationship of Earth to Sun, one twelfth of the period of rotation of the earth around the sun.

• YEAR – relationship of the Earth to the solar system, one rotation of the Earth around the Sun.

• CENTURY –
relationship of the Earth to the Universe, the move-ment of our solar system within the galaxy and the universe.

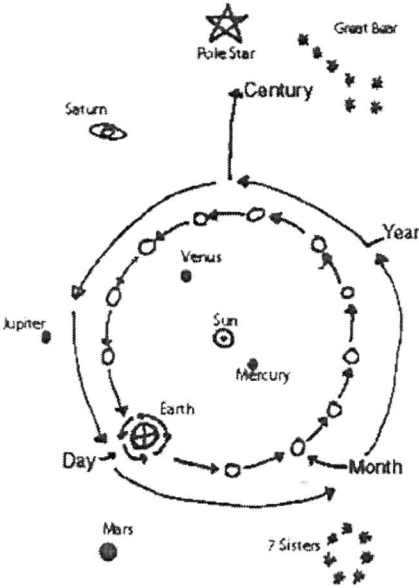

Conception Number

The other unchangeable is your conception number. It is the "thought-form" which describes your job for this incarnation. Most people don't know when their conception occurred but, occasionally, some do. If you or a friend is a reliable dowser you can find out this way. The best question system to ask is along these lines ...

1. Make a guess at when you were conceived by going back nine months. Add a week either side and ask ...

a. Was I conceived between X and Y? [give the dates you've reckoned]

b. If you get a YES go to 2 below, otherwise ask ... Was I conceived before X?

c. If you get a YES make another two-week period back from that date and ask the question at 1 again.

d. If you get NO ask ... Was I conceived after Y?

e. If you get a YES here (which you should do if you've had no up to now) make a two-week period forward from Y and ask the question at 1 again.

f. You should now have arrived where you can go to 2

2. For the period of days between X and Y list each day individually as shown here. Put your finger on the first date and ask "Was I conceived on [say the date, including the month and year]?". If you get NO go to the next date down. Continue until you get YES.

```
12
13
14
15
16
etc
```

Incidentally, if you want an astrological chart for your conception you can use the same technique to find the date, and adapt it slightly to find the time.

If, when dowsing, you get unclear answers this is because you are unclear yourself, you probably have too much emotional investment in the question. Stop. Wait until your emotional need has worn off before you dowse again.

The Number-Grid

The numbers grid is a way of writing down the numbers in a pattern so that you can see how they relate to the primal number.

```
      0
      9
8       1
7       2
6       3
5       4
```

Doing the numbers grid gives you the spread, like a hand of cards. You may find that you have none of one or two   numbers – all the examples lack some – but this doesn't mean you're a deformed person spiritually. Remember, you came in to do a job. You arranged your birthday so that you would have a particular set of numbers which would give you access to the qualities you need to do this job. Sometimes the lack of a particular tool can be just what you need. It can spark you in creative ways – like you don't have a screwdriver so you "manage" by using a knife blade. Your lack of a particular number may help you to empathise with others in a similar place. This doesn't mean they have to be lacking the same number as you. Just living with a "space" where you don't have a number gives you a different insight on to someone who does have some numbers in their hand. You can find yourself in sympathy with anyone in the same boat, even if the numbers they lack are different to the ones you don't have. And you may be able to offer them some insights or hear theirs.

A space is also a place waiting for some creativity, waiting for you to design into it, find out what it is, what it does. Knowing and working with your numbers is both complex and fun. You contain so much, all of which is useful.

You complete the grid like this …

• Write out the birth date separating the day, month and year as in the chart.

• Then add the numbers of each to reduce to a single figure. This gives you the flavour of each of them.

• Next, add the day and the month single figures together to give you the flavour of where in the year that person was born.

Day	Month	Century
26	5	1974
8		21
13		3
4		
7		

Year number
(19 + 74) = 93

• Now add the century number to the day-plus-month to get the actual birth number i.e. 4+3=7.

• Finally, add the 19 to the 74 to get the year number.

A completed numbers grid looks like this … each number from the chart is put by its number on the grid, plus the 9 and 3 of the year number.

You'll see that where there are more than one of any number I've put how many as a superscript. This gives extra information as you'll see in the examples.

	0		
$^{2}99$	9		
8	8	1	111^{3}
$^{2}77$	7	2	22^{2}
6	6	3	333^{3}
5	5	4	44^{2}

Name Number

This is the adjustable factor which you can shape and tune to best use the birth-power your soul built into you at incarnation.

Each letter of the alphabet is given a number, very simply, as below

A	B	C	D	E	F	G	H	I
1	2	3	4	5	6	7	8	9

J	K	L	M	N	O	P	Q	R
1	2	3	4	5	6	7	8	9

S	T	U	V	W	X	Y	Z
1	2	3	4	5	6	7	8

You write out the names, put the numbers for each letter underneath and add them, reducing down to a single number for each name. You then add these name numbers together and reduce them down to a single figure for the final name number.

You should take the name that you like to be known by and spell it that way. This is who you have chosen to be at this time. For interest later you can take the whole gamut of names your parents might have loaded you with and see what they come out to. This can change your mind about what you call yourself.

You use the number grid again to place the numbers so that you can see their relationships. Take this example ...

J O A N N E	D O N N E
1 6 1 5 5 5	4 6 5 5 5
23	25
5	7

(5+7)

12

(1+2)

3

Her name-numbers grid is ...

		0		
		9		
	8		1	111^3
7	7		2	222^3
$^2 66$	6		3	33^2
$^8 55555555$	5		4	4

We talk about what her numbers mean for her in the examples chapter.

Exercises

Body-Knowing
This is a useful technique and exercise for getting to know yourself and how to ask, of Otherworld, of your own body, of your subtle bodies ... indeed, ask of anything.

Body knowing is a technique humans have been putting aside for a very long time in the belief that the mind is the place of knowledge. This is true, the mind does hold knowledge. It also knows how to learn and discover things intellectually. Your body knows in a deeper, instinctual way. Every child knows this ancient technique ... until it is educated out of it by being grown up. And every animal. But what is it?

Think about a tree. Now, imagine telling someone from another planet what tree-ness is ... not what a tree looks like, not what it's made of, not what species it is, not where it grows. Try to tell them what tree-ness is. No analogies, no pictures, no "it's like a bush but bigger'. You have to *tell*, not show. Just about impossible?

But you *know*, intrinsically, what a tree is. You can recognise one. You'd probably have to resort to taking your extra-terrestrial friend out and showing them a tree, letting them touch the tree, smell it, hear its branches rustle, perhaps even taste it.

Notice, you resorted to the five bodily senses to get over what tree-ness is to ET?

You can use this method to know anything and it's extremely effective. Once your body knows something you won't forget it, it's there, always, and will come back to you instantly whenever you need it ... unlike your memory which often fails just at the inopportune moment.

An initial concept to take on board is that *everything* has life, soul and consciousness. Intellectuals call this "animism". Anima is a word for the soul, so animism is about knowing the soul in everything. As far as archaeologists can see it was the original ethos for human beings, they say evidence seems to support the idea that we all knew that all things have soul ... long, long ago. This idea has been shredded by just about all religions that came after and wish to make human beings the most important thing in creation. Saying only humans have souls is one way of doing this. These religions have further enforced uniformity by threats of dire punishment, in this world and any others, to those who don't believe as they do. This has had unfortunate consequences on human attitudes to, and treatment of, all life with whom we share this planet. It ranges through environmental stupidity, global warming, genetic engineering, agribusiness, cheap food, over-population ... the list is pretty long. So animism, knowing the soul in all things, can head us away from causing quite so much damage to our planet. It can also help enormously with knowing yourself.

Every cell in your body has a consciousness and a memory. It is *both* an individual and an essential member of a group – e.g. a cell in an organ, an organ of your body or your body itself – at the same time. Your body is an entity in its own right. As you know, it was created by your soul as a home for this incarnation. It was built out of the stuff, the matter, of this planet and that stuff will return to the planet when your soul leaves this incarnation and your body dies. Every atom, every tiniest piece of matter which makes up your body, has consciousness, and that consciousness holds knowledge and memory of everything that has happened to it.

All your experiences from birth to death are recorded in your cells' memory. Unsophisticated people, animals and children have natural access to this, they still know how to listen to this memory and information. You have experienced the insights you can gain through the simple exercise of drawing the numbers themselves and seeing what the body-actions of drawing show you.

The best and simplest way of accessing body knowing is to ASK but, for most of us, this requires letting go of a whole raft of preconceptions. Many, if not all, of these support our current self and world view, our current reality, and our intellect is terrified of letting go of them ... if we do, won't the world fall apart? That fear, lurking at the back of our brains, is one of the best stops for beginning the process of asking. Another fear is that we will look stupid, people will laugh at us, if we are even thought to be asking our body what it thinks of us changing our job or taking a lover. All of these are huge hurdles in the way of listening to our body-knowing.

So how do you learn to ask? Many people find this exercise effective.

BODY-KNOWING EXERCISE

Make a space for yourself where you won't be disturbed for an hour. It's good to make an offering to the four elements which make up life on this planet – earth, air, fire and water. You could use an oil burner, it incorporates all the elements – the clay pot for earth; candle fire for fire; the water which carries the oil; the scent of the oil for air. These burners also need topping up about every twenty minutes or so which should ensure you don't drift off for hours.

In focused meditations like this it's important to retain discipline. Your actual journey should be only about twenty minutes. For this purpose, I suggest you sit in a comfortable chair which supports your back, your muscles should be able to relax but you don't go to sleep. Again, don't do this work when you're tired, you need to be fresh and awake, it's a conscious consciousness process, not a dream.

Get yourself a glass of water, paper, pens, crayons, tissues (in case tears come or your nose needs blowing). Make sure you're warm and comfortable. Put a "do not disturb" notice on the door and turn off the phones. Put a clock where you can see it when you come back. Make sure no bright light or sunlight will hit your eyes and disturb you.

1. Take a piece of paper and write BODY on it.

2. Sit quietly and clear yourself of worries and thoughts, allow them to flow past you, like having the TV on but not watching it. Find yourself at a still point.

3. When you're ready, light the candle and put three drops of your chosen essential oil onto the water. As you do this, compose yourself and say aloud ...

I wish to learn body-knowing
I wish to learn body-knowing
I wish to learn body-knowing

4. Settle into your chair, feel yourself within your body, feel connected with it.

5. Ask Body, does it have anything it wishes to tell you? Any advice, words, phrases, pictures, senses, scents, images, gifts, for you? Spend the next fifteen minutes listening and hearing what Body has to say to you. Attend to Body.

6. As the time comes to a close, thank Body for being with you, for what it has told and given you.

7. Say [*and mean it*] that you will return to listen to Body again soon.

8. Say farewell.

9. Return to your everyday consciousness, in your own room. It's good to stretch, rub your hands, arms, legs, head, to remind yourself of your physical body and ensure your consciousness is within it again. Have a drink of water.

10. When you are ready, clear your thoughts and bring yourself back to your everyday consciousness. Make brief

drawings, notes, reminders, of what Body said to you and gave you.

11. When you're done drawing and writing, close the elements altar. Blow out the candle, saying thank you to the fire element; pour away the water, thanking the water element; breathe in the last of the scent and thank the air element; clean the oil burner thanking the earth element. This tidying process helps to put a boundary, an edge, on your journey so you don't have bits of it drifting about with you all over the place like an old cobweb.

12. Put your drawings and notes aside, look at them again tomorrow. For now, let your journey go into the Cauldron of the Unconscious, to brew.

I modify this exercise for all sorts of purposes, you may like to do the same.

You've now experienced listening to your body, asking it to tell you, show you, what it knows. Body often speaks to us through sensations, scents, feelings in our bones or our water, scalp prickling, weak at the knees, light-headed – you can call up the old sayings for yourself. Now you have an inkling of how they came about, you are beginning to re-member them for yourself.

Next day, take the notes you made in the Body Exercise and spend time with them. Do this in an easy way, curled on the sofa maybe, with a hot drink. Be alone. Resist all temptation to tell your friends and loved ones about your experience. Don't talk about it. This sort of experience needs time to brew, ferment, distil. It's like its counterpart, the physical spirit of an old brandy. Don't hurry it, don't open the vat and stir it, don't try to pour it for your friend until it's aged suitably.

So take your notes and ponder them in luxurious solitude. Pondering is another spiritual technique worth learning. To do it properly you have to send your intellect and your reasoning powers out to play for an hour or so. If you keep them with you they will wreck the whole process and you'll end up even more befuddled by reason than when you started out. So give them some virtual pocket money and send them off to play.

Set yourself up in a favourite, comfortable place, with your favourite drink, paper, coloured pencils/crayons and put the "Do not disturb" sign on the door. When you're sitting comfortably, pick up your notes and just hold them. Close your eyes so you can't be tempted to begin reading them.

You'll receive sensations in your body again. It might be as simple as hearing your heart beat, or your breathing. Whatever sensation you notice as you hold your notes, allow it to seep into you, go through you. Mentally note any images, words or phrases which come, or any apparent changes of light noticeable through your *closed* eyelids. There will come a moment when the experience "switches off". When this happens put the notes down and open your eyes.

Have a sip of that drink.

Using your coloured pens/crayons, make drawings and notes again to remind you of the sensations you've just experienced. Write the words in colour too. Deliberately, don't be neat, write words sideways and upside-down all over the paper. Let your hand choose where and how to draw and write. If you're right handed try letting your left hand do the drawing, and the writing. If you're left handed let your right hand do it. You are re-educating yourself to understanding when your body talks to you instead of dismissing it as an aberration as we are encouraged to do nowadays.

110

When you've done this, got your latest set of notes down on paper, pick up your first set and look at them. Try not to read at first, just look. It should be easier because you've woken and worked with your body, that's why I asked you to do those exercises before reading your notes. It's a way of getting your normal brain to go off-line, so freeing up space for your body to come on-line.

Have another sip of that drink.

• Look at your first set of notes, what patterns do you see in them?

• When you've got an idea of this, take the second set of notes and look at them. What patterns do you see? And what similarities are there in the patterns from the two sets of notes.

Take a third piece of paper and draw/write (in colour) the similarities you just found. Draw their pattern. Write their words. Then sit sipping that drink and contemplate this third set of patterns. Insights will come to you. As they do, roll their names, the words for them, around your mouth like a piece of delicious chocolate. Words, and the insights they carry, are as delightful as this. Savour them.

You can relish ideas and concepts like good food or a beautiful perfume. Nutrition of the senses, as Rudolph Steiner put it, although he didn't go quite as far as you and I are doing. By savouring, feeding your senses, you are putting all that experience into your cell-memory. By doing it to this sort of intensity you are enhancing your read-out mechanism so that you will be able to go back to your body and get a very realistic action-replay.

This is body-knowing.

Soul Contact

Name numbers define the outline and potential of your personality in the current lifetime in the light of the soul's purpose. Birth numbers are the blueprint for the home, the grail-cup, which the soul can inhabit in the current lifetime. The name number can be likened to the facilities of that home, the washing machine, computer, car, mobile phone, the furniture and decoration. All the things which help your soul to have a fruitful incarnation. If your name numbers don't enhance your birth number, perhaps even work against it, then it's like living in an inconvenient house with all the wrong facilities, furniture and decoration for the life you lead. You can change your name. With care and inspiration you can find a name which you like and which brings out and/or adds to the qualities your soul needs to do its job in the current incarnation.

How do you do this?

We discussed earlier how the soul decides on an incarnation and the job it wants to do in it, in concert with its soul-group. Most of us, on getting born are hit with a bad case of spiritual amnesia, we haven't a clue why we decided to come down this time. For a while, this is usually a good thing. If we knew what the whole plan was before our personalities are strong enough to hold that knowledge we would run out on the job. It would be too big, too much and too in our face. The spiritual amnesia allows the personality space and time to grow without knowing the full size and scale of the job, which would be a knockout. Also, knowing the job would change the choices we make in our lives, we would try not to make mistakes ... and those mistakes might well be vital to our learning!

However, there comes a time when we, the personality self, can choose to wake up and smell the coffee. We often read avidly at this time and may well become 'course junkies', but the work that works best is what we do ourselves. Other people's ideas and experiences are very useful, we can fill our Cauldron of Knowledge with them but we need to cook them into a suitable form for our own personal digestive system. And then we must learn to eat slowly, savouring each mouthful, chewing it properly, not gorging and allowing it to digest before we pack more in. All of these are difficult things to master.

We can learn to work directly with our own soul, our first master, the one who really does know why we're here. There's an old adage, *'You get more sense talking to the engineer than you do to the greasy rag!'*. Our soul is the engineer, everyone else is (in the nicest possible way) the greasy rag. It's not that they're stupid or malicious but the cannot know our soul's purpose for us, not even if they're the best clairvoyant in the whole world.

EXERCISE: CONTACTING YOUR SOUL

This exercise begins with the same process as the previous one. Make a space for yourself where you won't be disturbed for an hour. It's good to make an offering to the four elements which make up life on this planet – earth, air, fire and water. You could use an oil burner, it incorporates all the elements – the clay pot for earth; candle fire for fire; the water which carries the oil; the scent of the oil for air. These burners also need topping up about every twenty minutes or so which should ensure you don't drift off for hours.

In focused meditations like this it's important to retain discipline. Your actual journey should be only about twenty minutes. For this purpose, I suggest you sit in a comfortable chair which supports your back, your muscles should be able to relax but you don't go to sleep. Again, don't do this work when you're tired, you need to be fresh and awake, it's a conscious consciousness process, not a dream.

Get yourself a glass of water, paper, pens, crayons, tissues (in case tears come or your nose needs blowing). Make sure you're warm and comfortable. Put a "do not disturb" notice on the door and turn of the phones. Put a clock where you can see it when you come back. Make sure no bright light or sunlight will hit your eyes and disturb you.

1. When you're ready, light the candle and put three drops of your chosen essential oil onto the water. As you do this, compose yourself and say aloud …

> *I am ready to meet my soul*
> *I am ready to meet my soul*
> *I am ready to meet my soul*
> *Soul, I invite you to come in*

2. Then sit back comfortably in your chair and close your eyes.

3. Wait. Don't panic. Wait quietly and watchfully.

4. Observe every feeling and sensation in your body.

5. Be aware of your breathing and follow its rhythm.

6. Allow your excitement to calm down.

7. Your soul will come. It may or may not look like you expect it to. It will be wearing an appearance as you wear clothes, so that you will recognise and respond to it. The images and memories which its appearance brings to mind are important. Your soul is using these as part of its means of communication with you.

8. When your soul comes, ask it … *"Are you my soul?"*.

9. Ask three times, so you are sure.

10. Part of growing up spiritually is to learn not to go blindly galumphing off with the first Otherworld being who shows up. It's quite possible Otherworld will test you this way, and you should take it as a compliment if they do. It means they think you're growing up and so are worthy of testing. Your soul, too, will be pleased to see you ask.

11. When you know it *is* your soul ask it what it needs of you, right now, at this time.

12. Don't begin with a shopping list of your wants, nor a life-story of your joy and grief. Remember, your soul already knows all this. Adults ask the visitor what they need and put their personal wants on hold while they listen attentively. If you do this you'll be amazed to find that what your soul tells you will assuage your personal needs, and in ways you'd not even considered.

13. So listen to your soul.

14. You will probably be asked if you really mean it, that you are ready, and if you are willing for your soul to be in conscious contact with you every day now. Answer from your heart. Don't try to think of "right answers", that's the child's way not the adult's.

15. Your soul will, of course, know you are reading about Numerology so ask if it will help you to use this tool as means of growth. Have a conversation with your soul.

16. When the conversation draws to a close, thank your soul for coming and ask if it will now come and live in your conscious personality. If it says yes then work out between you how to do this. When you've got it, it will probably happen instantaneously. Don't assume the soul will come to live with you, ask, be polite.

17. Return to your everyday consciousness, in your own room. It's good to stretch, rub your hands, arms, legs, head, to remind yourself of your physical body and ensure your consciousness is within it again. Have a drink of water. Now, before anything else, draw, write words, to remind yourself of what happened, what you saw and, most particularly, what your soul told you. Drawings can be as good or better reminders.

18. When you're done drawing and writing, close the elements altar. Blow out the candle, saying thank you to the fire element; pour away the water, thanking the water element; breathe in the last of the scent and thank the air element; clean the oil burner thanking the earth element. This tidying process helps to put a boundary, an edge, on your journey so you don't have bits of it drifting about with you all over the place like an old cobweb.

19. Put your drawings and notes aside, look at them again tomorrow. For now, let your journey go into the Cauldron of the Unconscious, to brew.

Go over your notes each day, in a quite moment over a cup of tea. Add to them as they draw more images, words and phrases out of your mind. This is a process of getting to know yourself better, and your soul, joining them up as a working team.

Repeat this exercise in a few days. This time change your invocation to …

> *I would like to speak with my soul*
> *I would like to speak with my soul*
> *I would like to speak with my soul*

You still need to check, each time, that it is your soul who comes, don't be sloppy about this discipline. Over a period, which may take months, you'll become accustomed to your soul and, gradually, you'll find it feels natural and normal. In time, and don't rush it, you will find yourself ready to do the next exercise – moving to the seat of the soul.

EXERCISE: MOVING TO THE SEAT OF YOUR SOUL

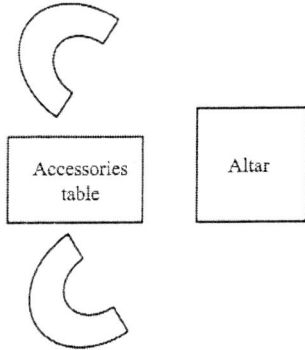

You need two physical chairs for this exercise. Set up an altar-focus, have representative symbols for the four elements on it. Use the oil burner again, which holds all four elements. Put any special objects you love onto the altar too.

Set the chairs side by side but with a forty-five degree angle between them, so you can see the other chair when you sit in either one, and you can see the altar. Leave space between the chairs and the altar so you can walk from one to the other.

Stand opposite the two chairs and look carefully at each. Ask, in your heart, which one you should choose to be the seat of your soul.

When you have discovered this ask the other chair if it is content to be your *personality-chair*. It may seem strange to you, at first, to be asking apparently inanimate objects if they are happy to work with you ... but everything in this universe has a consciousness, even if it isn't like yours, and everything works much better if you give it respect. Once you get into the habit of taking care of "things" you'll notice the difference. You don't have to talk about it with your friends if you feel they would laugh at you, you can do it in your mind/heart and no-one will notice.

117

Remember, focused meditations are a conscious consciousness process, not a dream, so it's important to retain discipline, not to drift off and not to journey too long, only about twenty minutes. You don't go to sleep so you need to be fresh and awake, don't work when you're tired.

Have an accessories table between the two chairs with a glass of water, clock, paper, pens, crayons, tissues on it. Make sure you're warm and comfortable. Put a "do not disturb" notice on the door and turn off the phones. Make sure no bright light or sunlight will hit your eyes and disturb you.

1. When you're ready, light the candle and put three drops of your chosen essential oil onto the water. As you do this, compose yourself and say aloud ...

> *I am ready to move to the seat of my soul*
> *I am ready to move to the seat of my soul*
> *I am ready to move to the seat of my soul*
> *Soul, come help me to make this change*

2. Then sit back comfortably in your personality-chair and close your eyes.

3. Wait. Don't panic. Wait quietly and watchfully.

4. Observe every feeling and sensation in your body.

5. Be aware of your breathing and follow its rhythm.

6. Allow your excitement to calm down.

7. Now ... get used to this chair, sense, feel, think and intuit what it is that defines your *personality-chair*, what it is that defines your personality.

8. Make some notes on these feelings.

9. When you've got the feel for the *personality-chair* ... ask your soul to come.

10. When your soul comes, check, ask ... *"Are you my soul?"*.

11. Ask three times, so you are sure.

12. Remember, your checking-process is part of growing up spiritually so don't neglect it. Gradually this will go on auto-pilot for you and you will naturally always check.

13. When you know it is your soul say that you wish to move to the seat of the soul.

14. Your soul will invite you to cross to its chair. Do so. This is a momentous journey, these few steps from your personality seat to the seat of your soul. Make the steps slowly, in full consciousness. Be aware of your body sensations as you make the crossing.

15. Now ... get used to this the *soul-chair*. How does it feel physically? What are the differences (and they may be quite subtle) between the sense of this your *soul-chair* and your *personality-chair*? What are the feelings, thinking and intuition like in this chair. Make some notes.

16. When you've got a feel for the *soul-chair*, move back to the *personality-chair* and see what this feels like now. Go through the sensory, feeling, thinking and intuitive functions again and make notes. There will be a difference now you've consciously sat in the seat of the soul.

17. When you have the updated feel for the *personality-chair* move back to the seat of the soul and sense into how it is to be here now. Move between the two several times, making notes of your sensations, feelings, thinking and intuition each time.

18. When you feel you've done moving between the two go to sit in the *personality-chair*. Look across to the soul-chair. How does it look from the seat of the personality? Make notes.

19. Now move again to the seat of the soul. Look across to the *personality-chair*. How does it appear from the perspective of the *soul-chair*.

20. Now see the chair as your personal self, view your personal self from the perspective of the soul. How does it appear? Do you find you love it more?

21. When you feel you are ready to return come out of the slightly altered state you will have been in whilst doing this exercise. You may notice that you felt extremely focused while doing it. This is normal and good but now you need to return to the more wide-angle lens view that you usually have when awake. Yawn, roll your tongue round your mouth, rub your arms and legs, body and head, convince yourself physically that you are here in the world. Have a drink of water.

22. When you're really back close the elements altar. Blow out the candle, saying thank you to the fire element; pour away the water, thanking the water element; breathe in the last of the scent and thank the air element; clean the oil burner thanking the earth element. Remember, this tidying process helps you put a boundary, on your journey, returning your whole self to the everyday world and not leaving cobwebs of yourself drifting between the worlds.

Take your drawings and notes to another place, preferably another room, and make yourself a hot drink. Settle quietly with your drink and the notes and look through them. Try to just look. Try not to get excited, not to correct or add things to them. Just holding them with your eyes shut will actually do a lot. When you've finished your drink put your notes somewhere safe to brew in the Cauldron of the Unconscious.

Look at them again tomorrow in a quiet place without interruptions and keep them secret to yourself

Make time to go over your notes each day. Now you can add to them as they draw more images, words and phrases out of your mind. This is a process of getting to know the seat your soul better, becoming accustomed to the view.

Repeat this exercise in a few days, changing your invocation to ...

I wish to know the seat of the soul
I wish to know the seat of the soul
I wish to know the seat of the soul

You need to check, each time, that it is your soul you are working with. Don't be sloppy about this. It may take you some time, perhaps months, until you become accustomed to the different perspective you have on life from the seat of your soul but, gradually, it will come to feel natural and normal.

6

Examples

Anny Wyse

BIRTH

Anny Wyse's birthday is 6-8-1948, so her birth number is 9.

DAY	MONTH	CENTURY	YEAR
6	8	1948	(19+48)
(6+8)		(1+9+4+8)	67
14		22	
(1+4)		(2+2)	
5		4	
	(5+4)		
	9		

I add the century/year number in two different ways, first for the century and secondly for the year. But you use the numbers 1, 9, 4, 8, only once in the numbers grid.

You put down the numbers on the grid in order, from left to right, like this ...

6, 8, 1, 9, 4, 8, 1, 4, 2, 2, 5, 4, 9, 6, 7
... excluding those in brackets.

Anny's birth number grid looks like this ...

	0		
^{2} **99**	9		
^{2} **88**	8	1	**11** ^{2}
7	7	2	**22** ^{2}
^{2} **66**	6	3	
5	5	4	**444** ^{3}

You see that Anny has no zeros, two 9s, two 8s, one 7, two 6s, one 5, three 4s, no 3s, two 2s, and two 1s. I've shown multiples of each number by putting a superscript 2 or 3 beside them ... i.e. Anny has 9 to the power of 2, 8 to the power of 2, 6 to the power of 2, 1 to the power of 2, 2 to the power of 2 and 4 to the power of 3.

Having two ones, one to the power of two, is different from just adding the ones together. For instance, the power of 1-ness in Anny's case is tinted with the power of 2. She does her 1-ness with a 2 flavour.

If you get more than one of any number it, or they, will be your secondary driver(s) after your main birth number. In this case, Anny has four numbers to the power of 2 and one to the power of 3, so her secondary drivers, after her birth number of 9, are 2 and 3. Let's explore her birth numbers chart.

Anny's birth number is 9. This means that her natural tendencies go towards the positive and negative qualities of the Void. She will be a powerful person and needs to learn to use her power appropriately. She will suffer all the temptations of 9-ness ...

• Being Invisible – liking this and wanting to hide; disliking it and feeling not seen and unappreciated.

• The Communicator – wanting to communicate with everyone and everything; being angry/upset when she's misunderstood.

• The Trickster – enjoying puns; seeking connections others don't see; enjoying riddles and probably poetry; leading people up the garden path; pranks; building people up only to knock them down; being slippery; quicksilver.

• Truth – knowing and seeing things easily and clearly; not understanding when others don't; hating hypocrisy and steamrollering those who practise it.

Anny is not likely to be successful at anything which requires "politics". Oh, she can see the political ways and means but it will choke her to practise them and she will probably despise politicians. If her power is focused on the good of everything rather than personal power, and it likely will be with the rest of her numbers, then she will have no patience with people who are out for themselves and have no wider or inclusive vision of the planet and humanity as a whole.

Anny has lots of numbers to the power of 2 – 9, 8, 6, 2 and 1. This means she will use the energy of these umbers with a flavour of 2-ness and that will be one of her saving graces as well as a challenge some of the time. 9 is not an easy number to be saddled with and, as you'll see, it is also her name number so it could easily lead her into being a black hole. It is extremely hard to encompass the chaotic powers of the void within the human personality however, it seems Anny's soul, and her soul-group, added some leavening to the difficult broth of her birth number to help her find her way to her soul-job. She does her 9-ness with a 2-flavour, so her feelings-self is able to add some humanity, but 9 is an aspect of the god of the underworld which is not an easy burden.

Human beings are not gods, nor are they meant to be. Gods are difficult to see, they always seem clouded in a bright darkness which fools our eyes or is so dazzlingly bright it blinds us. Fortunately, Anny has five numbers to the power of 2 giving her a strong emotional leavening. However, she has to be careful not to go overboard here either.

In her birth numbers Anny only has two 2s, so the main energy is not excessive except ... well, she has two 2s. This jumps the power of her feeling self by a couple of orders of magnitude over the base rate.

To recap so far ...

• Anny's birth number is 9, a difficult one for humans.

• She has 2, the feelings-self, quite strongly.

• She does five out of the eight different numbers in her birth chart to the power of 2, i.e. with a feelings-self flavour.

What else? Anny has 4 to the power of 3, so her intuitional self is worked through the thinking-self lens and her intuition is up three orders of magnitude over the basic rate. This is a very strong trait.

Anny's qualities are ...

• Power – which she can use to enable.

• The Power is qualified by the feeling self.

• A very strong intuitional nature which is qualified by her thinking-self lens. This gives her the ability to understand her intuition and to question it accurately.

The strong intuitional nature will also give Anny a powerful ability to understand animals, plants and the natural world. To those not blessed with this talent she could seem quite omniscient in this area. She might choose a career as a vet or a scientist but she would need to be very careful. The ability to understand the natural world brings with it the ability to perceive its pain when humans use it unthinkingly or cruelly. If Anny saw this she would likely go ballistic and find herself in deep trouble.

Additionally, Anny's dislike of hypocrisy combined with these intuitive qualities and focused through the mind mean she would see straight through political and humanistic arguments put up to justify cruelty. If I was advising her, I would endeavour to point her away from a scientific or medical career. She could do the work very well, but she'd never survive the politics and might slaughter her colleagues, verbally if not physically.

Anny's qualities are …

1   Anny's two 1s give her a strong grounding and good instinctual ability. This combined with her intuitive talents will probably be her most obvious qualities. She is able to sense things well. She will also love and use her body possibly in sports or dance, something physical and powerful. All of these qualities are focused through the feelings-self lens.

2   With two 2s and using 2 as the focus for most of her other numbers Anny has a very strong feelings-self. She probably has the ability to touch people's consciousness too.

3   Anny has no 3s in her birth number so her thinking-function is hidden and comes out through her intuition, for which it is the focus.

4	Her intuitive function is very strong and this is how Anny does her thinking. She sees the answer, then works backwards to find the process of how to get there. She does the process-finding work largely so she can explain what she sees to others, certainly not to convince herself.

5   Her 5 means she's able to be in touch with her causal body and, as the 5 is focused through the 1, the body-sensing-lens, she will stay grounded whilst still being able to see into the soul-world and see her soul-purpose through her personal ego. The other numbers suggest there may have been quite a tussle at some point between her personal self and her soul for who's perspective she was going to see through. She is able to hear and understand what her soul wants, what her soul-job is for this lifetime – if she tries. She will always need to take care her personal vision aligns with her soul-purpose. Her thinking-lens mode of working with her intuition could subtly twist things to suit her personal perspective if she allows her concentration to slip.

6   The two 6s give Anny a strong knowing ability. Again, aligned with her intuition this can be a formidable tool, how she uses it will again be qualified by the feeling-lens. There are two main hazards here, either caring too much or too little. The feeling-lens has its drawbacks, as do all lenses. Anny must learn to stand back from things, take deep breaths, count backwards to a hundred, anything to keep a real perspective.

7   The single 7 gives Anny the Love/Wisdom touch and this will help her hold the perspective on her feeling nature. Having just the one 7 it is used through the sensory-body-lens which is a good grounding force. Anny should be able to feel deeply, find a way to

explore these feelings and then be able to act appropriately. But, like us all, she cannot take herself for granted, she must work at this all the time. The 7 opens the way for the Consciousness Teacher and her intuition, knowing, ancestral connection and her 9-ness suggest this as her soul job.

8   Anny has a strong connection with the Ancestors, Otherworld. She probably has vivid and accurate past-life memories. Again she works her spirit connection through her feeling-self. If she trains herself she will be able to see the ancestral realms and bring back wisdom from there. Combining this with her intuitive abilities would be very useful and effective. As always, she must keep her feelings/emotional lens clean and bright or she will get into trouble.

9   9 is her birth number. This and the two 9s give Anny a strong connection to the void, the power behind all things, and again it is focused through the feelings-lens. This will be a difficult one to handle but will attract her more than anything else. The void both attracts and repels but, to someone with a strong and intelligent intuitive nature, a good connection to spirit and the ancestral realms, and some ability in knowing, the attraction is going to be stronger than the repulsion. Her intuition being focused through intelligence will mean she is likely to feel quite at home with the energy of the void, unafraid of chaos and likely to understand it. Putting this understanding across to others will be a test, the role of the Consciousness Teacher.

Anny has no **3**s. This means her thinking-self is hidden. She certainly has thinking ability, her intuition is focused through her thinking-lens, but this is secondary, not a direct number in her chart. She probably had a hard time at school, was unlikely to ever have been brilliant at exams or as a scholar, and I would doubt she has any desire to be an academic.

Having no 0s means she won't be a scintillating mirror to everyone she meets. She has the quality of being able to see through subterfuge, deliberate or unconscious, from the intuition and through the wise owl. But Anny will be subtle in her way of showing you she can see. Her Trickster element will come out here. It will probably be some time after she's said whatever-it-was that her hearers will realise that, far from complimenting them, she was actually being quite sarcastic. There will always be an acerbic quality to her, an edge to her humour and a delight in the ridiculous, which comes from the 9. Anny will not suffer fools gladly. But, because there are no 0s, people may not see this at first as she won't be reflecting back to them directly, it will come through darkly, through the 9.

Anny's number is 9. Her power aligned with her knowing and intelligent intuition, and focused through her feelings-lens, will inspirit her life.

On the job front I feel her soul-purpose is to be a consciousness teacher. This may well come out through writing or art and I imagine she has a garden or, at least, some very strong link with nature.

An interesting chart. Now we do her name, you'll see how this adds extra power, and difficulties, for Anny.

NAME

A	N	N	Y		W	Y	S	E
1	5	5	7		5	7	1	5

$$(1+5+5+7)$$
$$18$$
$$9$$

$$(5+7+1+5)$$
$$18$$
$$9$$

$$18$$
$$9$$

Anny Wyse's name number is 9, like her birth number, quite emphatically so in fact as each name itself adds down to. Also, the numbers which make each name are exactly the same although in a different order to each other. This emphasises the numbers even more. She has chosen 9 as the focus for her life.

Anny's name number grid looks like this …

```
                0
  ³999          9
  ³888    8     1    11111⁵
   ²77    7     2
          6     3
  ⁴555    5     4
```

Looking at Anny through her name numbers it's quite obvious she's a void-person. Likely she will be a loner and probably quite difficult to live with. She's unlikely to be a feminine woman although she will be very attractive. She probably frightens men off too … well it's quite a challenge living on

130

the edge of a black hole! The attraction will be that, when you actually look into it, the black hole is not empty but full of beautiful and incredible things. The drawback, to anyone attempting to live with her, will be keeping your balance on the edge and not being sucked in.

Anny wouldn't thank you for diving into her maelstrom and losing yourself in her, she'd be bored to tears and feel she'd lost a friend. If she was in a dark mood – and all those 9s can bring these on when things are not going well – she would feel you had betrayed her by losing yourself in her. 9-ness flows through everything Anny is and does, despite her name having a glut of 1s and 5s.

The end of the Celtic poem I quoted earlier fits Anny quite well ...

I am the womb of every holt
I am the blaze on every hill
I am the queen of every hive
I am the shield for every head
I am the tomb of every hope

I feel it expresses Anny, the culmination of her birth and name numbers. It's a weird, shadowy verse, like most Celtic poetry, but it hints strongly at the ability to be everything which we saw in her birth numbers. This is a shapeshifter quality which enables those who have it to experience how it is to BE another being than themselves without losing their own identity.

Birth and Name Grid

	0		
⁴9999	9		
⁵88888	8	1	1111111⁷
²77	7	2	22²
6	6	3	
⁵55555	5	4	444³

Putting Anny's birth and name numbers together on the same grid shows how her innate birth characteristics are enhanced by those of her chosen name.

Our birth number is something we can't change. It was chosen by the soul, in conference with our soul group, before our conception even, when the soul was planning its current incarnation. But we have complete control over our name number, once we reach adult age, and can change it however we wish. We don't have to stay with any of the names our parents gave us, or any names we acquire through marriage, unless we choose to. Our name number is under the control of our personality. Depending on how aligned our personal self is with the soul we can choose to align our name number so the two work well together, and it aids with our soul-job. I would say Anny is quite in touch with her soul and using her name to do just this.

Anny still has no direct zeros or 3s, her 6, 4s and 2 remain the same and she adds no new numbers to those already in her birth chart. This suggests that she feels, perhaps unconsciously, those numbers are what she needs to do her work. She has added to the ones which she feels will best enhance her abilities. The five extra 1s have increased her personality dramatically, and her incisiveness, to a potential danger point where she must watch out for ego and arrogance. She has significantly added to her soul contact abilities (5) which will help her put a brake on the ego and enable her to keep it harnessed into her soul-purpose. She has brought the 5 up to the power of 5 which, by bringing the number to the power of itself, adds extra enhancement to the 5-ness. She will seek out her soul-purpose and follow whatever happens and, with the increased personality strength, she will do it regardless of relationships, job or anything.

She has added another 7, bring it to the power of 2. As 2 is 7s partner they add together to make 9, a wholeness. 7 to the power of 2 strengthens Anny's ability to use it. this makes it even more likely she will be a consciousness teacher and use her 9s to empower this.

She has given her ancestral connection the power of 5 too, aligning it with soul-purpose. This link of 5 and 8 will enable her to keep in tune with her soul-purpose through her strong link to the ancestors. Anny has enhanced her ancestral connection through her name, bringing it up to the power of the soul-group energy, which is very useful. The ancestral realms have so much wisdom, if we can hear it, including how *not* to do things, how they've messed up in the past. If we can hear this, then it's possible we won't make the same mistakes again.

Like all strong personalities, Anny will have to watch out she doesn't shock or trample people out of wanting to hear her. On the other hand she must beware of the power of charisma. It's a useful thing, it can help people to hear you but you can also cast a spell over them, enchant them in a 'power-over' manner. This is not good. As Anny has a strong spiritual connection it would not be difficult for her to become a guru, people could put her on a pedestal. She needs to remember the only way off a pedestal is down.

Anny is an empowerer, this is her choice from emphasising her 9s. She can do this through the use of her intuition and her strong ancestral connection and will probably be a consciousness teacher of some kind because of the way she has put together her 2s and 7s to add to 9, the wholeness number. Perhaps she will be a modern-day shaman as this involves the ability to empower others.

Joanne Donne

BIRTH

Joanne was born on 21-11-1981, so her birth number is 6.

DAY	MONTH	CENTURY
21	11	1981
3	2	19
	5	10
		1

6

Year number

(19+81)=100

Her numbers grid is …

^{3} **000**	0		
^{2} **99**	9		
8	8	1	**111111111**^{9}
	7	2	**22**^{2}
6	6	3	**3**
5	5	4	

The first thing which hits you from Joanne's numbers grid is the quantity of 1s, 1 to the power of 9. Although she came in with 6 as her focal point it will be this large number of 1s which will dominate much of the way Joanne does things.

Joanne has nine 1s so her sense of ego will be very strong, and her sensory abilities will be marked. Whatever she does, it will be very practical and successful ... as long as she learns how to work with her ego.

She does her 1-ness through the lens of the void. This will be difficult as she has no immediate connection with her intuition. She has 5 to the power of 1 so will see her soul-purpose through the ego-lens. Additionally, the three zeros make her a particularly dazzling mirror. Because of her enormous sense of self she's unlikely to have an innate understanding of what this means and will have to learn it as she goes through life, and she's likely to feel misunderstood. She'll be a very strong, full-on, person. It will be good if she can find the love/wisdom and intuitive aspects to help her ground her abilities and her awareness of her self.

She will feel and know her own body well, and enjoy it. She could be very sexy and, again, will need to take care she doesn't use her attractiveness abusively or in an overly manipulative way. She could find this useful in her work, using her charisma to get what she feels is best for whatever she's doing and this is something she'll have to watch. With that many 1s she is going to have an ego the size of the planet. This may not be all bad, a strong ego makes a wonderful castle for the soul to inhabit ... as long as she doesn't imprison it, like Rapunzel, with all the direful consequences of that tale.

Joanne will have to learn how to use the strengths which 1 to the power of 9 brings, and not to fall into the traps. Her worst pitfall will probably be a tendency to know best. CG Jung used to say to his students, "Never know best and never know first". This is an excellent dictum and one which Joanne should paste all over her bathroom mirror and engrave onto her heart.

With 6 as her birth number, knowing will be a force in her life, but the illusions cast by the bright light of her personality will be a maze for her to find her way through. That goal of knowing, her birth number, will pull her very hard and she'll want to do it right. She'll be full of best intentions – another disastrous quality. Best intentions are one of the most attractive traps for all of us and 1 to the power of 9 is going to enhance that for her nine-fold.

There are two major killers in human personalities – knowing best and good intentions. Good intentions come from a desire to do good, to help, cure all ills, stop all strife, create harmony in the world. They blind the person to the bigger picture. Joanne's 1s are going to fire that up nicely. Knowing best compounds the problem because the one who knows best will never think to ask the recipient of their generosity what they really need. The result is usually poison, physical, emotional and/or mental.

Such an event actually occurred in India in the last century because the good-hearted persons didn't ask the people if they could actually eat wheat – the donors were able to eat wheat so they assumed everyone could and thousands of tons were sent to cover a famine. At that time the Indian population's stomachs were set to eat rice, the wheat bread they made caused terrible digestive problems. If the philanthropists had asked, listened and heeded the problem would not have occurred. This raises another problem the person who knows best has to overcome, an inability to listen and take heed of what they are told. All of these are downsides of 1-ness which Joanne will have to overcome.

9 is a difficult number for humans to work with. Anny has a much broader spread of numbers than Joanne which helps her retain balance. Joanne will feel a strong call to use the power of the ego through the void. Her thinking function to the power of 1 the ego, will make her believe she is able to understand it. She will believe she knows what she's doing because of the "I can" strength of the 1s and the emotional/feeling lens on the 9s.

However, Joanne doesn't have to fall into these traps. Her birth number makes her a 6-person, a potential wise owl, a knowing one. When she gets the hang of how to use her strong personality to *enable* good, rather than to do good, she will be able to *know* successfully. Knowing, as we've seen when looking at 6-ness, has its own difficulties. It's unlikely Joanne will suffer from the absent-minded professor stuff with all those 1s but she could well inundate her audience with far too much information, and so lose them. The 1s will give her great enthusiasm which will need careful driving so as not to get out of hand.

Joanne has one 6 – so she does her knowing with the flavour of 1-ness, her personality and sensing self again. She could be driven by this. 1-ness is about practicality, leadership, one-pointed-ness, focus and concentration so she needs not to become fixated in her knowing but always to listen. She will be single-minded about whatever she does, while she's doing it, so her friends may need to encourage her to get a life beyond whatever her passion is. The old adage of "*work hard, play hard*" fits Joanne.

Let's go through Joanne's numbers.

1   1 to the power of 9 gives Joanne a strong personality. She will be a strong leader, single-minded and able to carry her projects through to completion. The strength of 1-ness will hold its own handicaps and Joanne will have to be aware of her own motivation in order to avoid them.

2   Joanne has 2 to the power of 2 so she does her 2-ness with a feeling flavour. She will be less likely to allow her feelings to rule than Anny because of the strength of her ego. The 2s will help her empathise with those around her and be a potential leavening to the ego. She will need to take care she doesn't use her feelings,

as tantrums, to manipulate others to suit her ego-drives.

3   Joanne has one 3 so, again, she does 3-ness with the flavour of 1. Her thinking-self will be in tune with her ego-self which will help her reasoning powers. The drawback here is the tendency to push her thinking along the lines of the wants of the ego. It will be a subtle trap, well qualified by the "nosebest syndrome", knowing best, which she will have to see in herself before she can realign it. Once she has this under control her thinking will be a valuable tool.

4   Joanne has no 4s, this part of herself is hidden. When we come to her name you will see where she can find it.

5   She has one 5, again she's working through the 1-ness filter, it is her natural way to finding her causal self, her job-description for this incarnation. She touches into the needs of the Plan through her earthly and earthy self.

6   Joanne's birth number is 6. Inherently, she came into this incarnation to be a wise owl, a knowing one, but she set herself a serious task to do so. This probably means she-the-soul really wants to get knowing into her soul-bones this time around. We give our personalities a hard job when we really want to get something right. Joanne has the tools within her numbers to do a knowing-job very well, if she gets her act together.

7   Joanne has no 7s. The love/wisdom aspect of herself is hidden. When we come to her name numbers you will see where she can find 7-ness.

8   Her one 8 is the other half of her strong 1-ness, and she does 8-ness with a ego-flavour. Again she will need to be careful not to be autocratic in her dealings with the ancestors. But it also means she sees spirit through herself and does feel herself to be a part of it. There are two possible extremes here, first that she might feel everything is a part of herself rather than that she is a part of everything; and secondly she may feel unworthy, too ego-ridden and guilty to acknowledge she is a part of everything else. She may feel like a blot on the landscape. Neither of these two poles is useful either to her or to Otherworld, and Joanne needs to find a balance.

9   Joanne has 9 to the power of 2, she does her 9-ness through her feeling nature. This combination of the void-energy with the feelings self will be less easy for Joanne than it is for Anny. Joanne is not a 9-person and the chaos energies won't feel like home to her. Her strong 1-ness can be the antipathy to chaos becoming an extreme need for order which, if threatened, will become rigidity. Where Anny finds the void attractive, Joanne will be repelled. Seeing it through the emotional/feelings lens will exacerbate this. 9-ness will feel cold and inhuman which, of course, it is, although its inhumanity is not evil or nasty. Perhaps un-human would be a better word, not human. Joanne will find it very difficult to make or understand this distinction.

She will *feel* the power of 9-ness and may be tempted to emotional blackmail, to use her feelings to sway people into doing what she wants, perhaps by making them feel guilty. Her thinking self will be able to find reasonable arguments, weasel words, to support her emotional case and she will back that with the power from her 9-ness. A subtle and difficult pitfall.

140

0   Joanne has zero to the power of 3, so does her mirroring with a thinking flavour. This could very well be blunt and autocratic, so making it very hard for her listener to hear the truth from her, and defeating her own purpose. Joanne will need to work on this, again there are things in her name which will help.

Joanne is a fascinating person, with enormous potential and ability, if she will learn to realise that potential. In my years doing numerology one of the things which has been born in on me is that all people are fascinating if we will only look and see them properly.

NAME

Joanne's name numbers grid is ...

JOANNE	DONNE				
1 6 15 5 5	4 6 5 5 5			0	
23	25			9	
5	7	8	1	111^3	
12		7	7	2	222^3
3	^{266}	6	3	33^2	
	^{855555555}	5	4	4	

Joanne's name number is 3, her birth number is 6, 6+3=9, so, combined, they give her a real balance, the intellect of the 3 plus the knowing of the 6. When the birth and name numbers add to 9 they give a special power to the person and affirm the focused line of attention for the lifetime. Anny's numbers were all 9, giving her the focus of 9-ness for her incarnation. But they were straight 9s, not any of the pairs of numbers which add to 9, as Joanne's are. Consequently Anny's way of doing her life will be different to Joanne's.

Joanne's birth number (chosen by the soul) is 6, the wise owl number. Her name number is 3, the thinking, intellectual ability, the practicality of living the mortal life. The wisdom of 6 needs the 3 as the means of bringing its knowing to life. So Joanne has an excellent working system with her birth and her name numbers.

As we've seen, Joanne tends to extremes, it seems she needs them in order to be Joanne. There can be a tendency to feel that people should not have excesses, that it's somehow not spiritual, etc, but this is a simplification which tries to put people into boxes not their size and shape.

Remember this drawing? Both are balanced, one is simple, obvious, static, the other is a more complex, dynamic balance, a balance of unequal weights, of excess ... but both work.

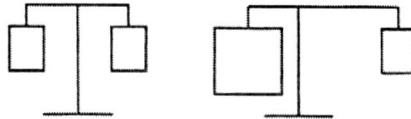

Looking at Joanne's birth and name grids shows where she carries her excess, and which powers she uses them with. In her name it is her ego-self, her sense of I-ness, of 1-ness. In her name it is her sense of soul-purpose and 5-ness. The soul needs the ego-self in order to function, it can't work if it has no ego to work through. The ego is like the "persona", the Greek word for the masks the actors wore which were known as the masks through which the gods could speak. We get our word personality from this ... so the personality is the mask through which the gods may speak. This gives quite a new light on the personality. No longer is it the villain of the piece, the bad-guy of our lives. Once we understand the concept of persona we understand its purpose, which is rather glorious ... to be the vehicle of the soul and the means by which the gods can speak and act in this world.

Joanne, through her birth and name numbers, has given herself the opportunity to do this. Her task is to get the 6 and the 3 working together, then that whole will be far more than the sum of its parts.

And what about all those 5s?

The eight 5s give her a strong incentive to discover her soul-purpose and they tell her where to look, in the ancestral realm, to go back and ask her soul group to remind her why she incarnated this time round. She holds this incentive in her name, the number she chose personally.

There's an interesting crossover here ... her soul chose the nine 1s of her birth number, while her personality chose eight 5s of her name number. So she comes to her soul-purpose through her personality and to her personality through her soul. An interesting way of working. To go through her name grid ...

1   Joanne has 1 to the power of 3, emphasising her name number and her practical thinking-self. She relates her ego to her thinking self. As always, she will need to take care not to fall into the traps of either 1 or 3, to use the 3-lens wisely, holding the idea of soul-purpose in mind. This will help stop her tripping over too often, but probably a few falls will be educational. It's never of the least use to try to get rid of the shadow, the shadow is what defines us and shows us where we are.

2   Again, in her name, Joanne has the 3-lens to do her feelings and her duality. This will help her *think* about

them and, in thinking, come to understanding. Wise owls need to think, as long as thinking doesn't rule. And it's good to think about the feeling-self as long as you still allow yourself to experience the feelings and don't intellectualise them.

3   Joanne uses her 2-lens to look at and work with her thinking-self. She does 2 through the 3-lens and 3 through the 2-lens and needs to be careful not to mix them up, not to do "I think I feel..." or "I feel that I think..".

4   Joanne gains the 4 she doesn't have in her birth numbers here in her name and so gets a handle on the intuition. This will help her find her soul-purpose.

5   Joanne's urge to discover her soul-purpose will be intense. She has just the one 5 in her birth grid, directing her towards her ego-self for this. Now, here, in her name, she has eight 5s. This shows that the place for her to discover it is through contact with the ancestral realm. Once she knows this, Joanne will become a person who can really help others. She may be a sage-type of wise owl, and looked on as an "elder" in the old sense of the word, a wise one who can help and advise. Or, if she uses the ego-path, she may become a guru who is worshipped. Like Anny, she needs to remind herself that the only way off a pedestal is down. Joanne's strong sense of individuality may make this distinction difficult for her to realise for a while.

6   In her birth grid, Joanne did her owl through the 1-lens, here in her name grid she does it through the 2-lens. Bringing the dream, the feelings, and the knowing of duality to her owlishness will be very valuable. She's unlikely to seem cold to people when

she says wise things and so they will be able to hear her. this strengthens her birth number and her owl is a gentle one.

7   Here is Joanne's Love/Wisdom aspect, in her name. It adds perspective to her feeling-self and to the feeling-duality lens she uses on several of her numbers. I said she might have difficulty with the power of the void, the 9, which she does through her 2-lens. The 7 energy will help with this. Where the feeling 2-ness can be overwhelmed by the void, Love/Wisdom will know how to work with it better.

8, 9   Joanne doesn't have these in her name. To use these
& 0   energies she must go through her birth number which she will be able to do once she has worked out her soul-purpose, through her name. The space allows room for personal growth and less focus on the void and the cauldron-mirror which may need to be more in the background for her until she finds her soul-purpose for this incarnation.

For Anny, the "big" energy numbers were very strong, although nowhere does she have the cauldron-mirror. The big energies are integral to her life and her soul-purpose. For Joanne they are not and she has to learn how to use them from the personality side. She's given herself he tools to do this too.

There's no right or wrong here. It's unwise to think some numbers are more spiritual than others and, therefore, more worth having. That's *either / or* thinking again and so contrary to the way of the universe. We all have many incarnations, each with different purposes for our own soul-growth and for how we can be useful in the Cosmic Plan. We take on different characteristics to suit each life, to aid our soul-purpose, to give us traits which are useful (even if we can't see how!) to the Plan and to our fellow workers, both human and non-human, physical and non-physical. We are all part of one whole and every one of us is different ... and necessary.

Joanne is only twenty-three as I write this book. In order to be an elder she needs life-experience, she needs to make mistakes, have successes, feel joy and pain, fall in love, be rejected, have wonderful relationships, build and grow her garden spiritually and physically. Her strong, independent and probably bolshy personal self will help her do this. She needs that pushy strength now, in her youth, to make sure she has space to live her own life rather than someone else's script. Only by doing this will she grow into the wise owl. Later, when she has a whole great trunk-full of experience and memories, she can invite others into her attic to find useful things for themselves. And she'll have the wisdom *not* to tell them anything but only give them stories from her life – like opening that experience-trunk and saying "help yourself".

Oscar Kane

BIRTH

Oscar Kane was born on 26-5-1974, so his birth number is 7

DAY	MONTH	CENTURY	His numbers grid is ...			
26	5	1974			0	
8		21	^{2}99		9	
	13	3	8	8	1	111^{3}
	4		^{2}77	7	2	22^{2}
		7	6	6	3	333^{3}
			5	5	4	44^{2}

Year number (19+74) + 93

Oscar's birth numbers grid shows he has a pretty even spread of numbers, nothing in excess and the only number he doesn't have is zero. He gets this in his name, as we will see. Both Anny and Joanne were skewed in their numbers, weighted in particular areas and showing obvious emphasis in certain directions. Oscar's chart is different. He has more numbers on the personality side but many people do, otherwise the initial view is much more balanced. A closer look shows he has four of his numbers to the power of 2, so there's a marked 2-ness flavour. His birth number is 7, the partner of 2, and this suggests he's working with his birth number. He also has 2 to the power of 2 so I feel he has a lot to learn about the feeling-self and its balance with love/wisdom.

Love/Wisdom, has its drawbacks as you know, a 7-person can become fixated that Love/Wisdom is *the* path. They can come to believe that duality is no good, look it with all the horror of old-fashioned perspectives on "the shadow". The consciousness teacher can slip into becoming the reformed sinner and proselytiser of *"The light! The light! And nothing but the light!"*. When they are well-mounted on this hobby-horse they can take some shifting before they understand the purposes and vitality of duality. My senses suggest that Oscar may have been such a one in a past life and that his soul has introduced this emphasis on 2-ness as an education in the shadow.

In tai chi you only stand with your weight evenly in both feet at the beginning and the end of the form, and at the end of each section. It is a static pose from which it is more difficult to move than when your weight is *balanced unequally*. In order to move from the Wu Ji you first have to transfer your weight from being evenly distributed in both legs to being concentrated in one of them. This is like walking ... taking that first *risk* to stand on one leg so you pick up the other and step forward.

Oscar's chart suggests a static balance rather than a mobile one and I feel that the emphasis on 2-ness is the piece of grit in his personal oyster which will make the pearl. Oscar has two 7s which will draw the Love/Wisdom, his soul's raison d'etre for this incarnation, into the labyrinth of duality. This is a journey which will refine it as well as making it very practical and visible in the everyday world. If there is a "sage on the mountain-top" itch within Oscar his 2-ness will draw that down into the everyday world where it can be of use to him and to others.

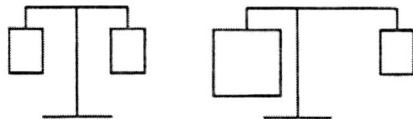

Oscar's challenges are different to Anny's or Joanne's. He is likely to appear strong, calm, together and so he is ... this is the challenge, to shift his weight into just one foot so he can lift the other and move forward.

Oscar will do well in a regular job. He can be the backbone of an organisation, someone to be relied upon. He may well be careful, painstaking, accurate and thorough. These qualities are easier for him because of his balanced, non-excessive set of numbers than they would be for someone with an uneven distribution. From his birth grid, Oscar is unlikely to be an inventor but he would be the person to bring the invention into a useful product in the marketplace. He would be very good at producing the drawings, project-managing the work, doing the business plan – things the inventor is probably far less able at.

With so many numbers to the power of 2, including the 2 itself, he will have a sensibility to others which will help him ease projects along. He will be able to see the emotional hitches and, provided he's on the ball and not in a messianic phase, see ways through them.

Let's go through his numbers ...

1   Oscar has 1 to the power of 3, so he does his 1-ness through the thinking/intellect-lens. He will be assured in his reasoning and may take the view of *I think, therefore I am.* He will be able to argue his case and be reasonable in getting his own way. As always with 1, he will need to take care to have other people's ideas and feelings on board, and also to add them into his own thinking before he makes a decision. He will be an able leader, with a good listening ear. The connection between his self-dom and his intellect is

quite strong. He has three 1s and three 3s, so the trap for him will be to "think" his path is the right one, for himself and everyone. Oscar could find it easy to walk the 1-rut, the singular path, becoming exclusive and so shutting out new ways of thinking.

2   Oscar has 2 to the power of 2 which emphasises his 2-ness. Any number to the power of itself accentuates its basic qualities. As I've said, I feel that Oscar's soul has brought in this emphasis on 2-ness to enable him to understand the purposes of duality, I and thou, relationships. Also to introduce the shadow so that he is able to define and know himself. Oscar's powers of empathy and sympathy should be quite good and his easy touch into all the numbers except zero will aid this. He can empathise with the characteristics of all the numbers. He may find himself pulled between feeling and thinking, into an *either/or* mode because he has two 2s and three 3s, each number being to the power of itself which makes it strong.

3   His 3 to the power of 3 adds an extra glow to the strength of his thinking self, so Oscar has 20/20 thinking and feeling. Using thinking and feeling of this quality is hard work and requires us to train for it, practice it and realise when we're getting it wrong. We have to go to the thinking gym and get the equivalent of a personal trainer to advise us. The exercises on contacting the soul and moving to the seat of the soul are useful here. The soul is our first master, our personal trainer, and far more useful than other human beings. They, like us, have to work through their personalities, with whatever lenses their soul designed in for them. There's no reason why we should lose our own critical faculties and follow their advice blindly. Yes, listen, add it into the pot, allow it time to brew, and then use it as best fits ourselves. Oscar will

need to train and hone his thinking abilities to ensure he doesn't bounce between this strong thinking and equally strong feeling, but finds a middle way where both are able to inspire and instruct him.

4   Oscar has 4 to the power of 2, uses his 2-ness lens on his intuitional abilities. He will need to take care that his feelings, desires, wants don't colour his intuition and so produce mirages. As always, there's a fine line here between allowing his intuition to be softened by his sensibility and letting his emotions run riot and rule the roost. If Oscar should go this way he'll leave himself open to subtle emotional blackmail, from his own self as well as others, which can be very difficult to see from inside. He may do things from a wish to be loved, approval-seeking, which is a downside of both 2 and 7.

5   The single 5 gives him a handle on his soul-purpose through his 1-ness lens, his personal ego and I-ness. He will need to be careful not to rationalise his soul-purpose into a box of a size his current ego can handle. There could be a tendency only to see so far here, not to want to stretch himself, and so miss out on what he's really come down for this time.

6   Oscar has the one 6, again using his ego-self-lens to do his wise owl. The same cautions apply for this as for 5 above. The personality alone doesn't get the full import of 6-ness, it needs to stay very open to learning if it's going to get the idea otherwise it will downsize the 6 energy rather than upsizing the personality. Only by growing and changing can we become wise, not by dumbing down to fit.

7   7 is Oscar's birth number and he does it to the power of 2, 7's partner. Oscar's soul really does seem to have

decided that its best means of growth this lifetime is through him learning duality. Love/Wisdom holds its energy in two apparent forms which could seem to be opposites. People tend to think of love as being a heart-thing and wisdom a head-thing, so separating them. This is a rational process and we often get caught up in thinking rational is real. As the song says, it ain't necessarily so.

Eastern traditions often call this world and our incarnations in it "the vale of illusion", which it is, after a fashion. The use of rationality as a measure for reality makes it so, for rationalisation cuts off great chunks of reality ... just as Cinderella's sisters cut off bits of their feet in attempts to make them fit the glass slipper so they could get the prince for husband. The result was that they went lame for the rest of their lives. So do we if we make a god of rational thinking and measure everything in life by this limited spectrum

Having 7 to the power of 2 offers Oscar the opportunity to get out of this box, to discover that love and wisdom are facets of one energy ... they, too, are a duality. Remember Ursula le Guin's story of the place of Unshadow, where the travellers could no longer see where they were because there was no shadow to define *this* from *that*.

8   Oscar has just the one 8. He sees the ancestral realm through the lens of his ego-self. This has two sides. Having one 8 gives a strong relationship to 1 as 8 is the partner of 1, but it's very subtle and easy to miss, like a flickering shadow. This subtlety is exacerbated by looking through the I-ness lens. The personality, for most of us, is a rational being, we're trained into this box from babyhood, all through school, university/

college, job-training and work. It's what makes economics work and we're all slaves to economics. So Oscar could miss the ancestral connection by looking at it rationally, which will make him believe it is unreal, explain it away as a sub-personality, inner world, etc.

If he's able to climb out of this rationality box, and see the ancestral realm as it truly is, it will be a wealth of learning, knowledge and knowing for him. It will really help him to understand duality and so integrate himself.

9   Oscar has 9 to the power of 2, as does Joanne. Where Joanne might well fear the void because of her personality make-up, Oscar is more likely to find it a nuisance, something which keeps turning over his carefully constructed universe which, of course, is one of the things chaos-energy does. Oscar has again given himself the duality lens to explore chaos with, perhaps through the coin of chaos/order and how destruction can enable creation. This could be deep stuff for Oscar but not beyond him by any means. It just might take him a while before he will allow it to teach him.

0   Oscar has left himself a space here, at zero. He fills it in his name grid as we'll see. He has no container or mirror energy through his birth grid. Neither does Anny and, as I've said, not having a number doesn't make you a spiritual cripple in that area. As Oscar seems to have given himself the task of learning duality in order to be able to work his soul-task of love/wisdom actually not having a cauldron (box) to hold himself together in is probably a good move. He will have to work at keeping his act together. Anny doesn't have the same problem as she's essentially a chaos-child, the whole universe is her container and she's quite happy with this.

Oscar is likely to pick at his *either/or* stuff like a scab on a wound when it begins to itch. But if he finds some sort of the 3rd position he'll come to a new place where he can real-ise *and/and*, the place of the triskele, the three-in-one.

NAME

Oscar's name number is 6, so his personality choice, whether conscious or not, is to be a wise owl. His soul's choice is to do the love/wisdom energy. These choices are by no means incompatible.

O S C A R	K A N E		0	0		
6 1 3 1 2	2 1 5 5		**9**	9		
20	13			8	1	**1111^4**
2	4			7	2	**222^3**
	6		^{2}**66**	6	3	**33^2**
			^{2}**55**	5	4	**4**

In his birth number Oscar has all the numbers except zero. Through his name he acquires zero but leaves himself space at both 7 and 8, love/wisdom and the ancestors. He brings himself no links to either of these through his choice of name but leaves himself room to grow into them.

In his birth number, I suggested that Oscar's chart is quite well balanced and that while this can be comfortable it can also be a rut. His name number shakes this comfort zone somewhat. Let's look at his chart.

1   Oscar now has 1 to the power of 4, he's doing his 1-ness through his intuitive self. This alone might

seriously move Oscar out of his steady state and into a more fluid way of being. If we add his birth and name 1s we get 1 to the power of 7, his birth number, If he can choose to work his ego-self through his birth number he could come to know himself from his soul's perspective. This would be good for his life, he would no longer be living it blindly but from the wider perspective of the one who created his personality. He might not know this at first but there is a strong chance he would get there, after all, his name number is that of *knowing*.

1 to the power of 7 gives him a very strong ego and there will be tussles here between the soul's purpose and Oscar's personal ideas. His birth chart has 1 to the power of 3, the intellect, reason. His name chart has 1 to the power of 4, the intuition which gives him a potential daring to follow his inner senses and connections to the universe. The 4+3 takes him to the love/wisdom energy, which needs a strong ego to contain it. The intuition will reach for the stars, way past the text-books and into the unknown. Oscar has put this together through his name so his unconscious, at least, would like to go there.

2   Oscar has 2 to the power of 3 in his name. He has reversed his birth number with his 2s and 3s. In his birth chart he had 2 to the power of 2 and 3 to the power of 3, each to their own power. Here, in his name, he swaps them about, does his feeling with his thinking-lens and his thinking with his feeling-lens. This could give him an interesting puzzle. It's quite likely Oscar may begin by mixing these two up so he may think how he feels and feel how he thinks ... not a good idea, in fact a recipe for misunderstanding himself and others.

At the time of writing this book Oscar is coming up to 30, a young man getting into his stride in life, in a relationship and a job. To intellectualise his feelings is going to make all these difficult. He could become a head-case and lose some emotional literacy and, because of his age, it's likely this will be the way of it at first. But he has a strong feeling-current running through his birth number so he will move through this phase eventually and come out with a better handle on his feelings.

Putting his birth and name numbers together gives him 2 to the power of 5, soul-purpose, so I feel Oscar will be heading to his soul-purpose through his feelings here. His soul-purpose is the 7, the love/wisdom, and he's given himself the link to see it, through his feeling-self.

3   His name gives him 3 to the power of 2, colouring his intellect with his emotions. Oscar is likely to be confused at first as to when he's thinking and when he's feeling. This will have been happening through his twenties, the 2-decade, and will probably reverse itself as he goes through his 30s, the 3-decade. He's likely then to use brain power on his feelings and cause himself, and everyone else, confusion.

Adding his birth and name 3s gives him 3 to the power of 5. Like with the combined 2s, he can do his thinking-self through the soul-purpose lens but it won't be easy at first and will shake Oscar's roots of convention. From his soul's point of view this is a good thing, growing through a confusion between thinking and feeling is useful for his soul-purpose.

4   In his name, Oscar has just the one 4, in his birth chart he has two.

Adding both his birth and name 4s gives him 4 to the power of 3, the thinking-lens again. He's likely to find thinking about his intuition an easy way to work with it, talking *about* it rather than actually exploring it. It's very easy to think about things and believe you are actually experiencing them, doing them in your mind … but you're not, you're doing them in your head and that is not reality. Oscar will go this way, at first.

There is a link between his name 4s and 1s. He has four 1s and one 4. This is the connection of his ego and his intuitive self through the "hall of mirrors" of thinking about intuition. He probably wont make this connection firmly until his forties (his 4-ness decade) but at that time he will probably see it.

This will be a space and time for him to get a handle on the intuition. He will have all the experience of his life so far to help him. Mistakes are just as valuable, if not more so, than getting it right. Oscar will be able to take a new look at himself and his intuitive abilities. They say life begins at 40 …

5   Oscar has 5 to the power or 2 in his name. In his birth chart he had one 5. He has reversed his 4s and 5s between his birth and his name. He has two 4s in his birth chart and one in his name. He has one 5 in his birth chart and two in his name. This swapping about is significant, he's done it before with the 2s and 3s and, each time, he gives himself fresh challenges. With his 4s he opened up a new window on the link to his intuition. With the 5s he emphasises his soul-purpose.

In his name, he does his soul-purpose through the feeling-lens but, when we add his birth and name 5s together we get three of them. this combination gives the thinking lens again, a difficult but potentially useful way of working.

When we looked at 3-ness we saw how it is able to put structure and form onto ideas, and feelings, giving us a means to transmit and share them. Oscar can do this here. The 3-lens has drawbacks and pitfalls but if he can get through those he will be able to show what he's learned to others. He doesn't have to talk, write or intellectualise but he will be able to show by being himself, by example. His soul-purpose, love/wisdom, is about consciousness teaching. Oscar seems to be giving himself quite a rigorous course in self-hood in order that, in his later life, he can show it to those around him.

6   Oscar has 6 to the power of 2 in his name and it is his name number. In his birth chart he had just the one 6. His name gives him the feeling-lens to do his wise owl through while the combination of birth and name brings the thinking-lens again.

His personality choice of 6, *knowing*, as his name number shows his personal self wants to *know*. His path to knowing is a hard one tempered here in his name by the feelings but again sharpened through the intellect when we put birth and name together, to get the whole person.

Oscar keeps giving himself this dilemma to solve, to sort out what feelings are and what thinking is, how they are different, how they help and support each other. This really does seem to be a theme for Oscar's life.

Knowing, the wise owl path, is what Oscar wants. He gives himself so many opportunities with this that I feel reasonably sure he will succeed, hopefully becoming a wise consciousness teacher.

7 & 8   Oscar's name gives space here. His birth gave him two 7s and one 8 so this is what he keeps with regard to existing influences. As he grows he will find his understanding of both love/wisdom and the ancestral really expand.

9   He has one 9 in his name chart and two in his birth chart ... yet again he gives himself the combined 3-lens.

9 is never going to be easy for Oscar, he is likely always to struggle to understand power and will probably fear it most of the time. The intellect encourages this with a potential *either/or* stance on power, either you are in control or you are controlled. To be able to be comfortable with power Oscar will need to move out of this ding-dong, pendulum place into a third position where he can understand power-to, the enabling power. I'm not sure he will do this. However the power will still be there, to enable him but he won't have a familiarity with it as Anny does.

As I said when discussing 9, it's an invisible power which we use through the qualities of our other numbers. It can be in-formed through reason, through the 3-lens, and expressed through the 2-lens, and these are Oscar's major lenses. It may be that the power of 9 will be well hidden by the intellect. The thinking-self is a very good screen to power, we think therefore we are and so we look no further for what drives us. It's probable that Oscar will go this way until middle life, then there may be an opportunity for him to change his perspective, something will happen after forty which will turn his life-view around, perhaps a mid-life crisis. His numbers suggest this.

Always such a crisis has at least two potential
outcomes and lots of others in between. We all set
ourselves tasks each incarnation which we can look at
through our birth chart. Then we modify and adapt
these by the choices we make in choosing our name.
Oscar has lots of potential for change as well as his
forty-something turn which I see from the 1-4
connection in his name. The power of 9 will drive these
whether Oscar is able to befriend 9-ness or not.

0   Oscar had no zero in his birth chart but gains one in
his name. The power of the mirror and the cauldron
will help him find ways through the challenges his
thinking lenses will bring up.

Like 9, this is an invisible number and yet it enables
everything. Without it we cannot move to another
decimal place in arithmetic operations, similarly we
cannot move ourselves to new levels of being without
the power of the zero.

Mirrors show us what we look like, enable us to see
ourselves. They also reflect light, will lighten a dark,
hidden area if placed there, and they help us to show
others how they appear too. This last is a dangerous
option, mirrors can distort as well as show truth, those
who have them need to learn how to use them and
Oscar will have to do this. Hopefully he will learn first
to look at himself but this will require him to let go of
comfortable images he will have built up. His strong 3-
ness traits won't like this.

The mirror will show the truth of the illusions and
disguises his thinking-self has built to make him feel
comfortable. He will have to dismantle these in order
to come at the truth of himself and this is never an
easy process. Like the 9, Oscar may fear the mirror

properties of zero and shy away from them. If he does this he will lose opportunities for growth and probably find it difficult to resolve his thinking. The structures that the thinking-self can put onto our lives can be very convincing and formidable, they provide a comfortable place for us to live without having to truly think very much … a paradox, but how it is. We follow along in the ruts of the life we know and don't want to move out. If the mirror shows them to be ugly, false and inappropriate we may well prefer to smash the mirror rather than see the truth.

The cauldron aspect of zero can be like a womb, also a very comfortable place where we don't have to act or think for ourselves but which provides all the nourishment and environment we need. Until birth-time. Then it rejects us, forces us out, we have to breathe air instead of getting our oxygen through fluid. There is light where we have only known the warm darkness. There is separation from the mother which has supported us and we eventually have to fend for ourselves. All of this will also be available to Oscar. He may choose to see and explore it, he may not. It is possible for a determined personality with a strong intellect to refuse birth and the soul never, ever forces us to become one with it, it waits until we choose from the personality side to sit in its seat.

What will Oscar choose? I don't know, but I hope he will go for it and get born, there is so much potential there.

Walking the Spiral Path

So...you have begun to walk the spiral path. It's a journey of discovery which can inspire your whole life, once our feet are on it, we don't turn back. Always, as you come to know yourself better, you want more - even the rough bits, the bad times, have more meaning when you understand better how the universe works...and that you are an integral part of it.

I wish you joy of your journey and, like Oscar, I hope you decide to go for it and get born.

Happy Birthday!

FREE DETAILED CATALOGUE

Capall Bann is owned and run by people actively involved in many of the areas in which we publish. A detailed illustrated catalogue is available on request, SAE or International Postal Coupon appreciated. **Titles can be ordered direct from Capall Bann, post free in the UK** (cheque or PO with order) or from good bookshops and specialist outlets.

A Breath Behind Time, Terri Hector
A Soul is Born by Eleyna Williamson
Angels and Goddesses - Celtic Christianity & Paganism, M. Howard
The Art of Conversation With the Genius Loci, Barry Patterson
Arthur - The Legend Unveiled, C Johnson & E Lung
Astrology The Inner Eye - A Guide in Everyday Language, E Smith
Auguries and Omens - The Magical Lore of Birds, Yvonne Aburrow
Asyniur - Womens Mysteries in the Northern Tradition, S McGrath
Beginnings - Geomancy, Builder's Rites & Electional Astrology in the
     European Tradition, Nigel Pennick
Between Earth and Sky, Julia Day
The Book of Seidr, Runic John
Caer Sidhe - Celtic Astrology and Astronomy, Michael Bayley
Call of the Horned Piper, Nigel Jackson
Can't Sleep, Won't Sleep, Linda Louisa Dell
Carnival of the Animals, Gregor Lamb
Cat's Company, Ann Walker
Celtic Faery Shamanism, Catrin James
Celtic Faery Shamanism - The Wisdom of the Otherworld, Catrin James
Celtic Lore & Druidic Ritual, Rhiannon Ryall
Celtic Sacrifice - Pre Christian Ritual & Religion, Marion Pearce
Celtic Saints and the Glastonbury Zodiac, Mary Caine
Circle and the Square, Jack Gale
Come Back To Life, Jenny Smedley
Compleat Vampyre - The Vampyre Shaman, Nigel Jackson
Creating Form From the Mist - The Wisdom of Women in Celtic Myth and
     Culture, Lynne Sinclair-Wood
Crystal Clear - A Guide to Quartz Crystal, Jennifer Dent
Crystal Doorways, Simon & Sue Lilly
Crossing the Borderlines - Guising, Masking & Ritual Animal Disguise in the
     European Tradition, Nigel Pennick
Dragons of the West, Nigel Pennick
Earth Dance - A Year of Pagan Rituals, Jan Brodie

Earth Harmony - Places of Power, Holiness & Healing, Nigel Pennick
Earth Magic, Margaret McArthur
Egyptian Animals - Guardians & Gateways of the Gods, Akkadia Ford
Eildon Tree (The) Romany Language & Lore, Michael Hoadley
Enchanted Forest - The Magical Lore of Trees, Yvonne Aburrow
Eternal Priestess, Sage Weston
Eternally Yours Faithfully, Roy Radford & Evelyn Gregory
Everything You Always Wanted To Know About Your Body, But So Far
        Nobody's Been Able To Tell You, Chris Thomas & D Baker
Experiencing the Green Man, Rob Hardy & Teresa Moorey
Fairies and Nature Spirits, Teresa Moorey
Fairies in the Irish Tradition, Molly Gowen
Familiars - Animal Powers of Britain, Anna Franklin
Flower Wisdom, Katherine Kear
Fool's First Steps, (The) Chris Thomas
Forest Paths - Tree Divination, Brian Harrison, Ill. S. Rouse
From Past to Future Life, Dr Roger Webber
Gardening For Wildlife Ron Wilson
God Year, The, Nigel Pennick & Helen Field
Goddess on the Cross, Dr George Young
Goddess Year, The, Nigel Pennick & Helen Field
Goddesses, Guardians & Groves, Jack Gale
Handbook For Pagan Healers, Liz Joan
Handbook of Fairies, Ronan Coghlan
Healing Book, The, Chris Thomas and Diane Baker
Healing Homes, Jennifer Dent
Healing Journeys, Paul Williamson
Healing Stones, Sue Philips
Herb Craft - Shamanic & Ritual Use of Herbs, Lavender & Franklin
In and Out the Windows, Dilys Gator
In Search of Herne the Hunter, Eric Fitch
In Search of the Green Man, Peter Hill
Inner Mysteries of the Goths, Nigel Pennick
Inner Space Workbook - Develop Thru Tarot, C Summers & J Vayne
Intuitive Journey, Ann Walker Isis - African Queen, Akkadia Ford
Journey Home, The, Chris Thomas
Kecks, Keddles & Kesh - Celtic Lang & The Cog Almanac, Bayley
Language of the Psycards, Berenice
Legend of Robin Hood, The, Richard Rutherford-Moore
Lid Off the Cauldron, Patricia Crowther
Light From the Shadows - Modern Traditional Witchcraft, Gwyn
Lore of the Sacred Horse, Marion Davies
Lost Lands & Sunken Cities (2nd ed.), Nigel Pennick
Magic For the Next 1,000 Years, Jack Gale
Magic of Herbs - A Complete Home Herbal, Rhiannon Ryall
Magical Guardians - Exploring the Spirit and Nature of Trees, Philip Heselton

164

Magical History of the Horse, Janet Farrar & Virginia Russell
Magical Lore of Animals, Yvonne Aburrow
Magical Lore of Cats, Marion Davies
Magical Lore of Herbs, Marion Davies
Magick Without Peers, Ariadne Rainbird & David Rankine
Masks of Misrule - Horned God & His Cult in Europe, Nigel Jackson
Medium Rare - Reminiscences of a Clairvoyant, Muriel Renard
Mind Massage - 60 Creative Visualisations, Marlene Maundrill
Mirrors of Magic - Evoking the Spirit of the Dewponds, P Heselton
The Moon and You, Teresa Moorey
Moon Mysteries, Jan Brodie
Mysteries of the Runes, Michael Howard
Mystic Life of Animals, Ann Walker
New Celtic Oracle The, Nigel Pennick & Nigel Jackson
Oracle of Geomancy, Nigel Pennick
Pagan Feasts - Seasonal Food for the 8 Festivals, Franklin & Phillips
Patchwork of Magic - Living in a Pagan World, Julia Day
Pathworking - A Practical Book of Guided Meditations, Pete Jennings
Personal Power, Anna Franklin
Pickingill Papers - The Origins of Gardnerian Wicca, Bill Liddell
Pillars of Tubal Cain, Nigel Jackson
Planet Earth - The Universe's Experiment, Chris Thomas
Practical Divining, Richard Foord
Practical Meditation, Steve Hounsome
Practical Spirituality, Steve Hounsome
Psychic Self Defence - Real Solutions, Jan Brodie
Real Fairies, David Tame
Reality - How It Works & Why It Mostly Doesn't, Rik Dent
Romany Tapestry, Michael Houghton
Runic Astrology, Nigel Pennick
Sacred Animals, Gordon MacLellan
Sacred Celtic Animals, Marion Davies, Ill. Simon Rouse
Sacred Dorset - On the Path of the Dragon, Peter Knight
Sacred Grove - The Mysteries of the Forest, Yvonne Aburrow
Sacred Geometry, Nigel Pennick
Sacred Ring - Pagan Origins of British Folk Festivals, M. Howard
Season of Sorcery - On Becoming a Wisewoman, Poppy Palin
Seasonal Magic - Diary of a Village Witch, Paddy Slade
Secret Places of the Goddess, Philip Heselton
Secret Signs & Sigils, Nigel Pennick
The Secrets of East Anglian Magic, Nigel Pennick
A Seeker's Guide To Past Lives, Paul Williamson
Seeking Pagan Gods, Teresa Moorey
Self Enlightenment, Mayan O'Brien
Spirits of the Earth series, Jaq D Hawkins
Stony Gaze, Investigating Celtic Heads John Billingsley

Stumbling Through the Undergrowth , Mark Kirwan-Heyhoe
Subterranean Kingdom, The, revised 2nd ed, Nigel Pennick
Symbols of Ancient Gods, Rhiannon Ryall
Talking to the Earth, Gordon MacLellan
Talking With Nature, Julie Hood
Taming the Wolf - Full Moon Meditations, Steve Hounsome
The Other Kingdoms Speak, Helena Hawley
Transformation of Housework, Ben Bushill
Tree: Essence of Healing, Simon & Sue Lilly
Tree: Essence, Spirit & Teacher, Simon & Sue Lilly
Tree Seer, Simon & Sue Lilly
Through the Veil, Peter Paddon
Understanding Chaos Magic, Jaq D Hawkins
Understanding Past Lives, Dilys Gater
Understanding Second Sight, Dilys Gater
Understanding Spirit Guides, Dilys Gater
Understanding Star Children, Dilys Gater
The Urban Shaman, Dilys Gater
Vortex - The End of History, Mary Russell
Warriors at the Edge of Time, Jan Fry
Water Witches, Tony Steele
Way of the Magus, Michael Howard
Weaving a Web of Magic, Rhiannon Ryall
West Country Wicca, Rhiannon Ryall
What's Your Poison? vol 1, Tina Tarrant
Wheel of the Year, Teresa Moorey & Jane Brideson
Wildwitch - The Craft of the Natural Psychic, Poppy Palin
Wildwood King , Philip Kane
A Wisewoman's Book of Tea Leaf Reading, Pat Barki
The Witch's Kitchen, Val Thomas
Witches of Oz, Matthew & Julia Philips
Wondrous Land - The Faery Faith of Ireland by Dr Kay Mullin
Working With Crystals, Shirley o'Donoghue
Working With Natural Energy, Shirley o'Donoghue
Working With the Merlin, Geoff Hughes
Your Talking Pet, Ann Walker

FREE detailed catalogue and FREE 'Inspiration' magazine

Contact: Capall Bann Publishing, Auton Farm, Milverton, Somerset, TA4 1NE